Dash Diet Cookbook for Beginners

Transform Your Health With Simple, Flavorful Recipes, for Lowering Blood Pressure and Boosting Your Well-Being

Kayla Patton

© Copyright 2024 - All rights reserved.

The content contained within this book may not be reproduced, duplicated or transmitted without direct written permission from the author or the publisher.

Under no circumstances will any blame or legal responsibility be held against the publisher, or author, for any damages, reparation, or monetary loss due to the information contained within this book, either directly or indirectly.

Legal Notice:

This book is copyright protected. It is only for personal use. You cannot amend, distribute, sell, use, quote or paraphrase any part, or the content within this book, without the consent of the author or publisher.

Disclaimer Notice:

Please note the information contained within this document is for educational and entertainment purposes only. All effort has been executed to present accurate, up to date, reliable, complete information. No warranties of any kind are declared or implied. Readers acknowledge that the author is not engaged in the rendering of legal, financial, medical or professional advice. The content within this book has been derived from various sources. Please consult a licensed professional before attempting any techniques outlined in this book.

By reading this document, the reader agrees that under no circumstances is the author responsible for any losses, direct or indirect, that are incurred as a result of the use of the information contained within this document, including, but not limited to, errors, omissions, or inaccuracies.

Table of Contents

Table of Contents	iii
Chapter 1: Introduction to the DASH Diet	1
The Consequences of Unchecked Indulgence	1
Pursuing Balance	2
The DASH Diet: Briefly Explained	2
The Benefits of a Healthy Lifestyle	3
What to Expect From This Cookbook	3
Chapter 2: Understanding the DASH Diet	5
The DASH Diet: A Brief Background	5
The Foundations of the DASH Diet	6
The Sodium Connection	7
Benefits Beyond Blood Pressure Control	7
Chapter 3: Getting Started With the DASH Diet	9
Tips for Transitioning to the DASH Diet	9
Stocking Up Your Kitchen	11
Foods to Avoid in the Dash Diet	12
Chapter 4: Breakfast Recipes	14
Mixed Berry and Chia Overnight Oats	14
Spinach and Feta Omelette	15
Avocado Toast With Poached Egg	17
Whole-Grain Banana Pancakes	19
Cottage Cheese and Peach Parfait	21
Spinach and Mushroom Breakfast Scramble	22
Quinoa and Black Bean Breakfast Bowl	24
Almond Butter and Banana Smoothie	26
Sweet Potato and Spinach Breakfast Hash	28
Savory Vegetable and Quinoa Bowl	30
Spinach and Ricotta Breakfast Wraps	32
Chapter 5: Lunch Recipes	34
Mediterranean Chickpea Salad	34

Grilled Vegetable and Quinoa Wrap	36
Turkey and Avocado Club Salad	38
Lentil Soup With Spinach	40
Roasted Vegetable Pita Pocket	42
Curried Chicken Salad Lettuce Wraps	44
Hearty Minestrone Soup	46
Tuna and White Bean Salad	49
Sweet Potato and Black Bean Burritos	51
Mediterranean Quinoa Salad Bowl	53
Lemon Herb Tuna Salad	55
Asian Chicken Salad With Sesame Ginger Dressing	56
Smoky BBQ Tempeh Wrap	59
Chickpea Curry Sandwich	60
Chapter 6: Dinner Recipes	**63**
Lemon-Herb Baked Salmon With Asparagus	63
Stuffed Bell Peppers With Quinoa and Black Beans	65
Herb-Crusted Chicken and Roasted Vegetables	67
Balsamic Glazed Pork Chops With Roasted Sweet Potatoes	69
Beef and Broccoli Stir-Fry	71
Spicy Garlic Shrimp With Quinoa	73
Rosemary and Dijon Mustard Baked Chicken	75
Maple-Glazed Salmon With Steamed Broccoli	77
Grilled Lamb Chops With Mint Yogurt Sauce	79
Tangy Baked Cod With Capers	80
Garlic and Lemon Roasted Chicken	82
Seared Scallops With Citrus Quinoa Salad	84
Veal Piccata With Steamed Broccoli	86
DASH-Friendly Sloppy Joe	88
Chapter 7: Snacks and Desserts	**91**
Cinnamon Apple Chips	91
Greek Yogurt Parfait	93
Savory Roasted Chickpeas	95

- Dark Chocolate and Almond Energy Bites ... 96
- Spiced Roasted Pumpkin Seeds ... 98
- No-Bake Peanut Butter Energy Balls ... 100
- Almond Oatmeal Cookies ... 101
- Avocado and Hummus Veggie Sandwich ... 104
- Coconut Chia Pudding ... 105

Chapter 8: Vegetable Dishes ... 108
- Roasted Brussels Sprouts With Balsamic Glaze ... 108
- Grilled Vegetable Quinoa Salad ... 110
- Eggplant and Chickpea Curry ... 112
- Portobello Mushroom Steaks With Herb Sauce ... 114
- Cauliflower Steaks With Turmeric and Garlic ... 116
- Zucchini Noodles With Tomato and Basil Sauce ... 118
- Butternut Squash and Black Bean Enchiladas ... 120
- Spicy Stir-Fried Tofu With Vegetables ... 122
- Balsamic Glazed Beetroot and Goat Cheese Salad ... 124
- Grilled Portobello Mushroom Burgers ... 125

Measurement Charts ... 128
Conclusion ... 130
References ... 131

Bonus

Kick-start your DASH Diet Journey with this Ultimate Bonus Guide!

Scan the QR Code below and receive your free bonus!

https://dashdietingforbeginners.ck.page/dash-dieting

Chapter 1:
Introduction to the DASH Diet

Dieting can certainly be rough. After all, who doesn't love food, right? And somehow, food just tastes so much better when we know it's bad for us. People often warn us that ice cream can lead to elevated blood sugar levels and obesity. Yet, it's still a beloved treat. Burgers and pizzas are abundant in empty carbohydrates and trans fats. However, society is in love with them! What a big dilemma! All the food that we love seems to be so bad for us.

It's true. Food can be a great source of comfort for many of us. When large groups of people congregate during meals, it presents an opportunity to bond and really connect with one another. People often associate food with their livelihood or cultural identity. As a species, our relationship with food has definitely evolved over the years.

Food was considered a daily necessity in the past. It was purely a source of sustenance. Our ancestors in the Paleolithic age foraged and hunted for food as a means of survival. There was nothing cultural or experiential about the food they consumed. It was all born out of necessity. But nowadays, food has become so much more. And this has led to many people overindulging and abusing the vast availability of food. We no longer have to hunt for the food we want to eat. We can simply pick up the phone, and a freshly cooked pizza will be at our doorstep within 30 minutes.

The Consequences of Unchecked Indulgence

Of course, there's nothing wrong with indulging in delicious food every once in a while. After all, that's part of our evolution as a human race. The creativity, passion, and love that we have poured into the way we prepare and eat food can certainly be beautiful and wholesome. But it's also important to stress that there is such a thing as overindulgence. It's very possible to have too much of a good thing, and that's where the main problem lies. In the best-case scenario, you might gain a couple of pounds over the course of a week as a result of overindulging. But the worst-case scenarios are significantly worse.

When you overindulge in food, you put yourself at risk of possibly contracting some very serious diseases or medical conditions. Eating too much food on a consistent basis can lead to the development of hypertension, diabetes, and obesity. In fact, this has become such a big problem that the World Health Organization declared in 2022 that one out of every eight people was living with obesity. That means that these people are at risk of contracting serious diseases or having their lives negatively affected as a result of being obese.

Pursuing Balance

Now, does that mean that we have to get rid of stuff like ice cream, cakes, chips, and burgers? Does that mean that we just have to eat boring, tasteless food all the time in order to stay healthy? Well, not necessarily. It's all about finding and establishing a balance. All around the world, people are adopting dietary programs with the mindset that they're restricting their eating and limiting their gastronomic experiences. To a certain extent, that might be true, but it's not a sustainable way of approaching eating. And it's certainly not the ideal way to build a healthy relationship with food. We should view diets as life enhancers, not punishments. We must be able to view our dietary programs as tools to promote wellness.

The goal of dieting isn't to promote misery or to make you feel bad about your food habits. Rather, the goal of dieting is to help you develop a more wholesome and healthy relationship with the food that you eat. Don't buy into the notion that diets are only made up of unseasoned, boring food. It's still very much possible for you to enjoy the food you eat while maintaining a healthy lifestyle at the same time. It's just a matter of knowing how to moderate the food that you eat and subscribing to a system that promotes healthy and delicious eating.

The DASH Diet: Briefly Explained

The DASH diet is unique because it takes a specialized approach that focuses more on a dietary program that promotes sustainable wellness. Dietary Approaches to Stop Hypertension, or DASH, primarily targets individuals seeking heart-healthy lifestyles. The National Institutes of Health, in response to a growing global hypertension problem, developed the DASH diet, making it unique. There are many diets that typically focus on quick weight loss schemes, whereas the DASH diet is more of a sustainable eating plan that's designed for overall health and wellness.

While the DASH diet is certainly an incredibly nuanced meal plan, it can essentially be defined as a dietary pattern that is rich in fruits, vegetables, whole grains, and lean proteins. It also limits the consumption of sodium, sugar, and fats, all of which contribute to hypertension and heart disease. The approach isn't entirely about reducing salt intake or abstaining from eating ice cream for its sake. It's about establishing food habits that lead to long-term weight management and improved heart health.

We'll learn more about the foundational principles of the dash diet in the next chapter. There, we will delve deeper into the science behind the diet and why so many people have found it effective as a sustainable dietary program.

The Benefits of a Healthy Lifestyle

Life is a multifaceted experience that has so many complex elements, variables, and sensations that accompany it. And as we pursue the quest of living life to the fullest, it's important that we don't neglect the value of being well and pursuing a healthy lifestyle. You may not realize it, but the dietary choices that you make daily can have a profound impact on your physical health, mental capacity, and emotional well-being. Whether you follow the DASH diet or not, maintaining an active and healthy lifestyle should always be a priority.

Nourishing the Body

At its core, the DASH diet is about providing the body with the nutrients it requires to function in an optimal manner. The diet focuses on whole foods that are rich in vitamins, minerals, and fiber. Aside from that, it discourages the consumption of processed foods that are high in sodium and unhealthy fats. Ultimately, the only food recommended under the principles of the DASH diet should directly support the body's essential functions. This nutritional strategy helps stabilize blood pressure, reduce cholesterol levels, and manage blood sugar.

Energizing the Mind

More than just nourishing the body, adopting a healthy body has a way of enriching and energizing the mind. Studies have shown that foods rich in omega-3 fatty acids, antioxidants, and various vitamins all contribute to improved cognitive function (Jennings, 2017). These are exactly the kinds of benefits that you can expect from adopting a DASH diet, which promotes the regular consumption of these nutrients. In addition to that, limiting the consumption of sugar and fatty food items can also contribute to more stable moods and energy levels, which translate to higher levels of productivity.

What to Expect From This Cookbook

This book is more than just providing you with information on the DASH diet; it also functions as a cookbook. It's not enough that you simply learn about the science behind the diet. You have to know how to execute it in an actionable and practical manner. What use is theoretical knowledge when you don't have a plan of action for how to apply it in your everyday life? That's the reason why, aside from talking about the science of the DASH diet, this book is also going to provide you with easy and simple recipes from which you can borrow inspiration.

In the first parts of this book, we'll break down the principles of the DASH diet into easily digestible segments. This foundational knowledge is critical for you to understand the reasons for the diet plan. Next, we will discuss a variety of carefully crafted recipes that align with the guidelines and principles of the DASH diet. Of course, these recipes aren't just going to be bland chicken breasts and lettuce over and over again. The dishes that we'll compile in this book are designed to be delicious and diverse, so that you never get bored or disappointed with the food that you're eating. This way, you're more likely to stick with the diet for the long haul.

This cookbook will provide you with detailed nutritional information in addition to detailed preparation instructions for each dish. That way, you know the exact nutritional makeup that you're getting out of every dish. These details will help provide you with a more thorough understanding of what you're eating and how your body benefits from it.

More than anything, this cookbook seeks to be as easy and accessible as possible. So many people are discouraged from adopting healthy habits because they fear that the world of wellness is just too complicated. And it's true that there are those in the industry who have a tendency to overcomplicate such simple concepts. With the DASH diet, we're going back to basics. We'll be covering just the basic principles of good nutrition so that you never have to worry about being confused or lost. And the recipes that we'll include in this cookbook reflect that commitment to simplicity. You won't have to worry about being some kind of master chef or culinary expert. Even basic cooking knowledge will suffice to execute the dishes in this cookbook to absolute perfection.

Ultimately, prospects are bright. You might think that adopting a healthy diet is time-consuming, inconvenient, or even expensive, but that couldn't be farther from the truth. As you go through this book and its recipes, you will come to discover that eating healthy on a regular basis doesn't have to be expensive or complicated at all. It's all just a matter of feeding yourself with the right information and learning to incorporate these details into your life.

So, consider this the start of a wonderful journey of health and fitness for you moving forward. The path to a healthier you is paved with delicious food and creative dishes that you will never get bored of. With this cookbook, you will come to learn that being healthy has never tasted this good!

Chapter 2:
Understanding the DASH Diet

Starting a diet plan without understanding how or why it works would be like taking a college class without knowing whether it's relevant to getting your college degree. Sure, it might do you some good, but it might not necessarily help you meet your larger goals. The DASH diet is renowned for its effectiveness in lowering blood pressure and fostering overall wellness. But beyond that, what else do you know about the DASH diet? Again, it's important for you to truly understand what the DASH diet is about, how it works, and, most importantly, how it could potentially help make your life better.

In this chapter, we're going to go over a brief overview of the origins of the diet and how it has gained popularity in modern times. We'll also discuss the foundational principles of the diet and the science behind why it works. By taking the time to learn more about the nuances that make up this complex and revolutionary diet, you will be able to better align your dietary practices with your larger health and wellness goals.

The DASH Diet: A Brief Background

While there are no concrete dates that signal the official founding of the DASH diet, its roots can primarily be traced back to the early 1990s, when researchers began to explore the impact of dietary patterns on blood pressure levels (Challa & Uppaluri, 2023). The National Institutes of Health developed the diet to help the general population reduce blood pressure without medication, as previously mentioned. Published in the mid-1990s, the initial study demonstrated that a diet rich in fruits, vegetables, and low-fat dairy foods, with reduced saturated and total fat, could significantly lower blood pressure.

This served as a transformational period in the field of nutritional science. Never before had non-pharmacological solutions been provided as a way to lower blood pressure systematically. Hypertension happens to be an incredibly serious disease that millions of people worldwide struggle with. It's also a leading risk factor for heart disease and stroke.

The diet was so effective in its goal of regulating blood pressure that it managed to draw the immediate attention of those in the health and wellness community along with the general public. From there, further studies into the principles of the DASH diet were conducted. In fact, a DASH-Sodium study movement took place, whose efforts indicated that conflating DASH principles with reduced sodium intake could amplify blood pressure regulation efforts (Mandal, 2010).

More and more evidence came out supporting the principles of the DASH diet, which ultimately led to a drastic increase in its popularity. Endorsements from health organizations and dietary experts certainly added fuel to that fire as well. The DASH diet is incredibly simple in its essence and has made it more accessible for different kinds of people. Of course, the DASH diet isn't necessarily a new diet plan either. It has proven itself to be more than just a *fad* diet that comes and goes like fashion trends. More than anything, what sets the DASH diet apart is the fact that it doesn't necessarily offer a prescriptive approach to food. Rather, it emphasizes the importance of food groups, which allow for variety and flexibility. This has resulted in DASH being a more sustainable and encouraging choice for many people who are looking to get serious about their diets.

Many people today recognize the DASH diet as one of the most practical and effective eating plans for anyone looking to manage hypertension and promote good heart health.

The Foundations of the DASH Diet

One of the main reasons that the DASH diet is so effective is that it's relatively simple and easy to follow. Ultimately, these basic components serve as the foundation of this diet.

- **Fruits and vegetables:** High in potassium and fiber, which are pivotal for lowering blood pressure and maintaining a healthy digestive system.

- **Whole grains:** Whole grains keep you full longer, support heart health, and are an excellent source of energy and fiber.

- **Lean proteins:** Proteins such as fish, poultry, and legumes are essential for muscle building and repair without the unhealthy fats.

- **Low-fat dairy:** Dairy offers calcium and protein, which aid in strengthening muscles, joints, and bones.

- **Reduced sodium intake:** Lowering sodium consumption can have a significant impact on blood pressure levels.

- **Limited sweets and saturated fats:** Reducing sugars and saturated fats manages calorie intake and reduces the risk of cardiovascular disease.

Again, if you will notice, the DASH diet doesn't necessarily promote specific food items. It focuses more on proper allocations for food *groups*. So, if a person doesn't necessarily like eating bananas or broccoli, that's fine. There are other fruits and vegetables that still fall under DASH guidelines. For those who are looking to build lean muscle, the DASH diet also technically allows for the consumption of whey protein supplements, which other diet plans might not be tolerant of.

The Sodium Connection

It wouldn't be right to tell the story of the DASH diet without touching on its connection to sodium, a mineral that's found predominantly in table salt. This mineral plays a vital role in human physiology, as it helps with hydration, fluid balance, and nerve function. With that being said, consuming too much sodium can also be bad, as it's closely linked to high blood pressure and other cardiovascular illnesses. As a result, the DASH diet emphasizes food items that are naturally low in sodium. Let's delve deeper into how sodium, while good to a certain extent, can ultimately be bad for your body.

Sodium's Impact on Blood Pressure

Sodium does a great job of keeping you hydrated by holding water in your body. Yes, your body needs to stay hydrated, and this fluid balance is critical for the normal function of your vital organs. However, consuming too much sodium can also increase your blood pressure. This translates to your heart having to work harder and this increased pressure can strain your arteries' walls. So, while sodium is good for you, it's also possible to have too much of it.

As a way to counteract increased sodium content, one of the DASH diet's primary foundations is reduced sodium intake. The American Heart Association promotes a sodium intake of less than 2,300 milligrams per day (intext citation required). For adults with high blood pressure, the recommended sodium intake is 1,500 milligrams per day. By adopting the principles of the DASH diet, people are able to have better control over the potentially harmful effects that excess sodium consumption can have on the body.

Benefits Beyond Blood Pressure Control

Throughout this chapter, we've emphasized how the DASH diet is primarily a diet plan that seeks to promote better blood pressure management. Although the primary goal of the diet's development was blood pressure control, it also offers additional health benefits.

Enhanced Heart Health

Aside from lowering blood pressure, which yields positive impacts on the heart, the DASH diet also helps lower *bad* cholesterol. The diet discourages the intake of saturated fats and cholesterol, both of which are known to put people at risk when it comes to heart disease and stroke. On top of that, the DASH diet is incredibly nutrient-rich, which also promotes good heart health.

Weight Management

Weight management is one of the most common reasons anyone would ever adopt any kind of diet. That's why diet plans like intermittent fasting, or keto diets are so popular nowadays. They primarily promote themselves as a weight-loss diet. While the DASH diet isn't strictly a weight-loss diet, it does aid in the weight-loss process as well. The DASH diet promotes high consumption of fiber and lean protein, both of which can lead to a higher metabolism and weight loss. Fiber and protein also tend to leave people feeling satisfied for longer, which can reduce the desire for snacking in between meals.

Reduced Cancer Risk

Many diets aim to combat cancer as a whole, as it is one of the most common deadly ailments in society today. The DASH diet is rich in fruits, vegetables, and fiber, all of which contribute to a lower risk of certain types of cancer. The food items in these food groups contain antioxidants and phytochemicals, which may help protect cells from damage that can lead to cancer development.

By now, you should already know that the DASH diet offers a holistic approach to health and wellness. Originally designed to combat high blood pressure, it has evolved into much more than that. The diet lays the foundation for a healthier lifestyle overall. In the next chapter, we're going to talk more about the practical approaches to adopting the DASH diet into your life and ensuring that you're doing things right.

Chapter 3: Getting Started With the DASH Diet

If you've reached this point of the book, you're probably already convinced of the prowess of the DASH diet and how it can positively impact your life. While you may be eager to begin the diet, there is an optimal approach to follow. It's not just a matter of choosing DASH-friendly dishes and immediately incorporating them into your life. There's a method to all of this. And if you're truly interested in maximizing the benefits of this diet plan, it's essential that you take the time to approach things strategically.

Of course, adopting or transitioning to a new diet can be incredibly daunting and confusing. However, it doesn't always have to be. Health and wellness don't have to be as complicated as we make them out to be. In this chapter, we're going to cover all the essential tips and tricks that you need to know in order to ensure a smooth transition. We will provide you with practical advice on how to easily stock your kitchen with DASH-friendly food, ensuring you never experience hunger during this diet. Moreover, we'll also talk about the foods that you should avoid. Yes, the DASH diet isn't necessarily as restrictive as other diets out there. But there are still certain restrictions that we must follow in order to make the most of this diet plan.

Part of being successful in having a sustainable dietary journey is ensuring that you are minimizing the roadblocks and hazards to success. That's primarily what this chapter is for. We want to make the process of dieting as easy and convenient as possible so that we have very little to no reason to abandon or discard it so easily.

Tips for Transitioning to the DASH Diet

Whether you're dieting for the first time in your life or if you're transitioning from another diet plan, there's absolutely nothing for you to worry about. The DASH diet is as simple as diets come. In order to make the most of your experience adopting the DASH diet, here are a few things to be mindful of:

Assess Your Current Eating Habits

Before you start on a new diet, try to assess your current eating habits. This will offer you a baseline insight into what you're doing right and what you could possibly improve on. Start by keeping a food diary for even just a week. Record everything you eat and drink, noting the times of day and portions. This practice will help you identify patterns and areas for improvement.

Once you have analyzed your food habits, compare your findings regarding your current intake with DASH guidelines. Note how much you're consuming in terms of fruits, vegetables, lean proteins, and whole grains. Also, if possible, record your sodium intake. This isn't necessarily hard to do in the digital age. There are so many apps out there that will allow you to track the nutritional content of the food you eat.

Set Reasonable Dietary Goals

Any diet that you have should serve some kind of goal or purpose. Otherwise, you wouldn't have any motivation to stick to the diet at all. Before you even start the diet, make sure that you set goals for yourself with regard to your diet. Maybe you have the goal of lowering your blood pressure to fall within a recommended benchmark. Perhaps, you have the goal of lowering your daily sodium intake, or you're looking to manage your weight effectively. Whatever the case, having goals such as this is crucial for finding success with your diet.

Implement Gradual Changes

Completely adopting a new diet plan from scratch can be incredibly overwhelming, especially if it's so different from your usual eating habits. That's why it would be best to take a gradual approach if a radical one just isn't practical for you. If you don't really eat fruits or vegetables all that often, take a gradual approach to integrating them into your diet. Add one fruit or vegetable to every meal or snack until it becomes completely normal for you. That way, you're giving yourself a chance to acclimate yourself to this new diet plan.

Manage Your Cravings Effectively

When on a diet, unnecessary snacking is your enemy. It's important that you learn how to differentiate between a craving and genuine hunger. Next time you crave something unhealthy like a cookie or a slice of pie, think to yourself: wouldn't you rather have an apple instead? If the answer is yes, then go and have an apple to satisfy your hunger. If the answer is no, then you're probably not hungry, and you're just looking to satisfy your craving. Always be more mindful of the way that you consume your food.

Stay Hydrated

Get rid of those sugary juices or sodas that do nothing for you nutritionally. Yes, the DASH diet encourages you to consume fruits in their natural states. Turning fruits into juices has a tendency to strip away the essential nutrients, leaving only sugar. Juices also make it easy for you to overconsume, particularly the sugar that comes with fruits.

And you probably already know how unhealthy and sugar-laden sodas can be. When you're thirsty, it would be best to stick to water, especially if you live an active lifestyle.

Stocking Up Your Kitchen

Making sure that your kitchen has all the essential ingredients and food items necessary to stay consistent with your diet is absolutely essential. Having a well-stocked kitchen simplifies your approach to meal preparation and will make it easier for you to stick to your dietary goals.

Essential Foods to Have

- **Fruits and vegetables:** Aim for a colorful variety. Fresh produce is ideal, but frozen varieties can make for more economical and practical options. Think leafy greens, berries, apples, carrots, and bell peppers.

- **Whole grains:** Stock up on whole-wheat pasta, brown rice, whole-grain bread, quinoa, and oats. These food items provide essential fiber and nutrients.

- **Lean proteins:** Include a variety of lean protein sources such as chicken breast, turkey, fish, legumes (beans and lentils), and tofu.

- **Low-fat dairy:** Choose low-fat or fat-free dairy products like milk, yogurt, and cheese for your calcium and protein intake.

- **Nuts, seeds, and Legumes:** Almonds, walnuts, sunflower seeds, and flaxseeds are great for snacks or adding to meals. Beans and lentils are excellent protein and fiber sources.

- **Healthy fats:** Good fat sources like olive oil and avocado provide healthy monounsaturated fats. While being healthy, they can also be high in calories. So, make sure to use these ingredients for cooking and dressings in moderation, especially if you're watching your weight.

- **Herbs and spices:** Build a collection of salt-free seasoning blends, herbs, and spices to add flavor to your dishes without extra sodium.

Grocery Shopping Tips

- **Be mindful of the labels:** One good way to ensure that you're not eating sodium-rich food is to read nutritional labels before buying them. At the same time, watch out for hidden sugars and unhealthy fats, even in products marketed as healthy or organic.

- **Do meal planning:** Before shopping, plan your meals for the week. This helps you stay disciplined as it prevents you from buying items that don't fall within your plan.
- **Avoid processed foods:** Whenever possible, opt for whole foods over processed food options. That way, you get a better idea of what exactly goes into your dishes.

Foods to Avoid in the Dash Diet

Again, the DASH diet isn't necessarily very restrictive, but there are still certain restrictions that you must adhere to if you're going to find success. There are just certain food items that will potentially counteract your efforts to lower blood pressure and improve heart health. Let's go over some examples of such food:

High-Sodium Foods

Processed foods: Many canned soups, frozen dinners, and snack foods are high in sodium, even if they don't taste particularly salty. Instead of these, go for fresh or frozen alternatives without added salts.

Cured and deli meats: Food items like bacon, sausages, hot dogs, and deli meats often contain significant amounts of sodium as a preservative. While you may indulge in these items in moderation, it's always best to stick to fresh meats.

Condiments: Soy sauce, ketchup, mayonnaise, salad dressings, and other condiments can be surprisingly high in sodium. Look for low-sodium versions, or instead, use natural herbs and spices to flavor your food.

Saturated Fats and Trans Fats

Red meat: Limit consumption of beef, lamb, and pork, which are higher in saturated fats. Choose lean cuts and remove visible fat when you do eat them.

Full-fat dairy products: Full-fat milk, cheese, and cream can contribute to the intake of saturated fats. Switch to low-fat or fat-free dairy options.

Sugary Sweets and Beverages

Sugar-laced snacks: Cakes, cookies, candies, and pastries are high in sugar and often contain unhealthy fats, contributing to weight gain and increased blood pressure.

Sugary beverages: Sodas, fruit juices, sweetened teas, and coffees can significantly increase your blood sugar levels without necessarily providing you with any nutritional benefits.

For the past few chapters, we've covered practically everything that you need to know to get started on the DASH diet. We've laid the foundation, and it's time to start layering bricks on top of it. Hopefully, the recipes that you will find in the remainder of this book will bring as much joy to your soul as it will to your tastebuds. Remember that dieting doesn't have to be depressing. You just have to know how you can get creative with the food that you eat while understanding what your limitations are.

Chapter 4:
Breakfast Recipes

As they say, breakfast is the most important meal of the day. Having a good breakfast can help you feel more energetic and fuller throughout the day. In contrast, having poor or no breakfast at all could potentially lead you to feel sluggish and tempt you to overindulge in snacks throughout the day. The recipes that we will list in this chapter are designed to help you start the day off with the right food. They should provide you with just enough energy to help you power through the first parts of the day while also leaving you fuller and more satisfied for longer.

Mixed Berry and Chia Overnight Oats

This delicious breakfast requires a little preparation before bedtime, but that also means you can just immediately grab a spoon and dig in the moment you wake up! These overnight oats offer the fiber that comes from oats and chia feed blended together with the vitamins and minerals from the berries for a refreshing and healthy morning treat. It's a relatively simple dish to make, and it's perfect for those mornings when you're in a hurry and want something quick and ready.

Serving Size

- 2

Preparation Time

- 10 minutes

Cooking Time

- Overnight soaking in refrigerator

Ingredients

- 1 cup rolled oats
- 1 tablespoon chia seeds
- 1 cup low-fat milk or plant-based milk alternative

- 1/2 cup mixed berries (fresh or frozen)
- 1 tablespoon honey or maple syrup (optional)
- 1/2 teaspoon vanilla extract

Instructions

1. Combine rolled oats and chia seeds in a large bowl.
2. Stir in the milk, vanilla extract, and salt. Add honey or maple syrup for sweetness (optional)
3. Fold in the mixed berries.
4. Evenly distribute the mixture into two mason jars or containers with lids. Seal and let sit in the refrigerator overnight or for at least 6 hours.
5. Before serving, stir well.
6. Serve chilled, topped with additional fresh berries if desired.

Nutritional Information per Serving

- Calories: 350 kcal
- Total Fat: 5 g
- Saturated Fat: 1 g
- Cholesterol: 5 mg
- Sodium: 80 mg
- Total Carbohydrates: 60 g
- Dietary Fiber: 10 g
- Sugars: 15 g (includes 5g added sugars if using honey/maple syrup)
- Protein: 15 g

Spinach and Feta Omelette

With all of that spinach he was eating, Popeye was on to something. When it comes to your diet, adding a splash of color to your plate is rarely a bad idea. This particular green, leafy vegetable dish is packed with proteins, antioxidants, and healthy fats. It's incredibly flavorful and offers a hearty start to your day.

Serving Size

- 1

Preparation Time

- 5 minutes

Cooking Time

- 10 minutes

Ingredients

- 2 large eggs
- 1/4 cup low-fat milk
- 1 cup fresh spinach, roughly chopped
- 1/4 cup crumbled feta cheese (low-fat option preferred)
- 1/2 teaspoon olive oil
- salt and pepper to taste

Instructions

1. Whisk together the eggs, milk, salt, and pepper in a medium-sized bowl.
2. Heat olive oil in a non-stick skillet over medium heat. Add the spinach and sauté until just wilted, about 1-2 minutes.
3. Pour the egg mixture over the spinach. Sprinkle the oregano or fresh herbs evenly over the top.
4. As the eggs begin to set, gently lift the edges with a spatula and tilt the pan to allow the uncooked eggs to flow to the edges.

5. When the omelette is mostly set but still slightly runny on top, sprinkle the crumbled feta cheese over half of the omelette.

6. Once the cheese has slightly melted and the omelette has cooked to your liking, carefully fold it in half and continue cooking.

7. Slide the omelette onto a plate and serve immediately.

Nutritional Information per Serving

- Calories: 250 kcal
- Total Fat: 15 g
- Saturated Fat: 5 g
- Cholesterol: 380 mg
- Sodium: 400 mg
- Total Carbohydrates: 4 g
- Dietary Fiber: 1 g
- Sugars: 3 g
- Protein: 22 g

Avocado Toast With Poached Egg

You might be one of those who rolls your eyes at millennials and their obsession with avocados, but there's actually a lot of merit to the regular consumption of this fruit. Not only does it contain heart-healthy fats, but it also serves as an incredibly versatile ingredient for creating delicious meals. By pairing the fruit with a poached egg and bread, you're getting fats, proteins, and carbohydrates in a deliciously wrapped package.

Serving Size

- 1

Preparation Time

- 5 minutes

Cooking Time

- 10 minutes

Ingredients

- 1 large egg
- 1 slice of whole-grain bread
- 1/2 ripe avocado
- Salt and pepper to taste (optional)
- A sprinkle of crushed red pepper flakes (optional)
- A few leaves of fresh arugula or spinach (optional)
- A drizzle of olive oil (optional)

Instructions

1. Place a pot of water over a stove and bring to a slight simmer.
2. Crack the egg into a cup and gently slide it into the simmering water. Poach the egg for about 4 minutes for a soft yolk or longer for a firmer yolk. Remove with a slotted spoon and set aside.
3. While the egg is poaching, toast the whole-grain bread to your preferred level of doneness.
4. Mash the avocado in a bowl and season with a pinch of salt (optional) and pepper. Spread the mashed avocado evenly over the toasted bread.
5. Place the poached egg on top of the avocado spread. Season to taste with salt and pepper, and add red pepper flakes for a spicier flavor.
6. For a touch of green, garnish with fresh arugula or spinach leaves, and drizzle with olive oil for an extra layer of flavor.

Nutritional Information per Serving

- Calories: 330 kcal

- Total Fat: 20 g

- Saturated Fat: 4 g

- Cholesterol: 185 mg

- Sodium: 350 mg

- Total Carbohydrates: 27 g

- Dietary Fiber: 9 g

- Sugars: 3 g

- Protein: 13 g

Whole-Grain Banana Pancakes

In many households, breakfast is synonymous with pancakes. Unfortunately, a lot of people douse their pancakes with calorie-laden syrups and sweeteners that aren't good for us. Also, a lot of these grocery-bought, ready-to-make pancake mixes are filled with preservatives and other ingredients that might not be good for you. But that doesn't mean that you can't have pancakes for breakfast anymore! Make a delicious pancake dish from scratch to kickstart your day. This particular recipe is rich in fiber and potassium from the bananas while also offering a sweet and satisfying way to wake up in the morning.

Serving Size

- 2 (around 3 pancakes per serving)

Preparation Time

- 10 minutes

Cooking Time

- 15 minutes

Ingredients

- 1 cup whole-grain wheat flour (or any whole-grain flour of your choice)

- 1 tablespoon baking powder
- 1/4 teaspoon salt (optional; you may omit it for a lower sodium option)
- 1 ripe banana, mashed
- 1 cup low-fat milk or a plant-based milk alternative
- 1 egg
- 1 tablespoon honey or pure maple syrup (optional, for a touch of sweetness)
- 1/2 teaspoon vanilla extract
- Olive oil or cooking spray (for the pan)

Instructions

1. In a large bowl, whisk the whole-grain flour, baking powder, and salt together (if using).
2. In a separate bowl, combine the mashed banana, milk, egg, honey (or maple syrup), and vanilla extract until well mixed.
3. Add the wet ingredients to the dry ingredients and stir until just combined; it's fine if the batter is lumpy. To ensure fluffy pancakes, avoid overmixing.
4. Warm a non-stick skillet or griddle over medium heat and lightly oil it with olive oil or cooking spray.
5. For each pancake, pour 1/4 cup of batter onto the skillet. Cook until bubbles appear on the surface, then flip and cook until the other side is golden brown, about 2–3 minutes per side.
6. Serve warm with your choice of toppings, like fresh fruit, a spoonful of low-fat yogurt, or a drizzle of honey or pure maple syrup.

Nutritional Information per Serving

- Calories: 320 kcal
- Total Fat: 5 g
- Saturated Fat: 1 g

- Cholesterol: 95 mg

- Sodium: 200 mg (without added salt)

- Total Carbohydrates: 60 g

- Dietary Fiber: 8 g

- Sugars: 12 g

- Protein: 12 g

Cottage Cheese and Peach Parfait

Who doesn't love cheese? And we're not talking about the kind of overly processed cheese that's completely devoid of any nutrients. We're talking about delicious cheese that offers a creamy and satisfying texture to go along with sweet peaches and toasted oats. This particular breakfast recipe is high in protein and essential nutrients while being low in sodium. However, if you have a lactose intolerance, you might want to move on to another recipe, as cottage cheese has around 9 grams of lactose in a single serving cup. On the other hand, if you know that your stomach can tolerate it, then this is definitely a breakfast treat that you don't want to miss out on.

Serving Size

- 1

Preparation Time

- 5 minutes

Cooking Time

- No cooking required

Ingredients

- 1/2 cup low-fat cottage cheese

- 1 ripe peach, sliced (canned peaches drained of juice is also permissible)

- 1/4 cup rolled oats, lightly toasted

- 1 tablespoon chopped almonds (optional)
- honey and cinnamon to taste (optional)

Instructions

1. If you're using rolled oats, lightly toast them in a dry skillet over medium heat until golden and aromatic. Once toasted, allow them to cool.
2. Place half of the cottage cheese in the bottom of a serving glass or bowl.
3. Layer half of the sliced peaches on top of the cottage cheese.
4. Sprinkle half of the toasted oats and almonds (if using) over the peaches.
5. Layer the remaining cottage cheese, peaches, and oats or almonds.
6. Finish with a drizzle of honey or a dash of cinnamon for extra sweetness, if desired.
7. For the best texture, enjoy immediately, or chill for up to an hour before serving.

Nutritional Information per Serving

- Calories: 280 kcal
- Total Fat: 4 g
- Saturated Fat: 1 g
- Cholesterol: 10 mg
- Sodium: 350 mg
- Total Carbohydrates: 42 g
- Dietary Fiber: 5 g
- Sugars: 22 g (natural sugars from peach and optional honey)
- Protein: 20 g

Spinach and Mushroom Breakfast Scramble

For our breakfast options, spinach makes a comeback. But instead of pairing it with feta cheese, we're going to go for another ingredient that provides more texture and deeper flavors: mushrooms. This particular dish is perfect for DASH diet followers as it is packed with delicious vegetables that offer fiber, vitamins, and minerals that all promote a healthy heart. The lean protein from the eggs also aids in muscle preservation and strengthening, especially for those who lead relatively active lifestyles. Eggs also have a tendency to make you fuller for longer, so you are less likely to indulge in unnecessary snacking before lunch.

Serving Size

- 2

Preparation Time

- 5 minutes

Cooking Time

- 10 minutes

Ingredients

- 4 large eggs
- 2 cups fresh spinach, roughly chopped
- 1 cup mushrooms, sliced
- 1/4 cup red bell pepper, diced
- 1/4 cup onion, finely chopped
- 2 tablespoons low-fat milk (or a plant-based milk alternative)
- 1/4 teaspoon black pepper
- 1/2 teaspoon olive oil
- 1 tablespoon low-sodium cheese (optional), grated
- Fresh herbs (such as parsley or chives), for garnish (optional)

Instructions

1. In a bowl, whisk together the eggs, milk, and black pepper until well combined.

2. Heat olive oil in a non-stick skillet over medium heat. Add the onions and red bell peppers, sautéing until softened, about 2–3 minutes.

3. Add the mushrooms to the skillet and cook for approximately 3 minutes, until they start to release their moisture and become golden.

4. Stir in the spinach and cook until just wilted, about 1-2 minutes.

5. Pour the egg mixture over the vegetables in the skillet. Let it sit without stirring for about 1 minute, then gently scramble the eggs with the vegetables until the eggs are fully cooked but still moist, about 2–3 minutes.

6. If using, sprinkle the low-sodium cheese over the scramble just before removing it from the heat, allowing it to melt slightly.

7. Divide the scramble between two plates and garnish with fresh herbs if desired.

8. Optional tip: Feel free to add other DASH-friendly vegetables, such as tomatoes or zucchinis, to this dish for added texture and flavor.

Nutritional Information per Serving

- Calories: 220 kcal
- Total Fat: 12 g
- Saturated Fat: 3 g
- Cholesterol: 370 mg
- Sodium: 200 mg
- Total Carbohydrates: 8 g
- Dietary Fiber: 2 g
- Sugars: 4 g
- Protein: 20 g

Quinoa and Black Bean Breakfast Bowl

As you have already learned, the DASH diet puts an emphasis on dishes that incorporate whole grains and legumes. These ingredients offer a good blend of protein, fiber, and complex carbohydrates, all of which promote overall health and wellness. Aside from being good for you, this particular recipe is going to appeal to those with savory preferences as a way to start the morning.

Serving Size

- 2

Preparation Time

- 15 minutes (if starting with cooked quinoa)

Cooking Time

- No additional cooking time required (if quinoa is already cooked)

Ingredients

- 1 cup cooked quinoa (cooked according to package instructions)
- 1/2 cup black beans, rinsed and drained (low-sodium canned or cooked from dry)
- 1 small avocado, sliced
- 1 cup cherry tomatoes, halved
- 1/2 cup fresh spinach, chopped
- 2 tablespoons fresh cilantro, chopped (optional)
- 2 tablespoons green onions, sliced
- Juice of 1 lime
- 1/4 teaspoon ground cumin
- Salt (optional, to taste) and pepper to taste
- 2 tablespoons low-fat Greek yogurt (optional, for serving)

Instructions

1. In a large bowl, mix the cooked quinoa with black beans. Season with lime juice, ground cumin, salt (optional), and pepper until thoroughly combined.

2. Distribute the quinoa-bean mixture equally into two bowls.

3. Garnish each bowl with sliced avocado, cherry tomatoes, chopped spinach, cilantro (optional), and green onions.

4. If you like, accompany each serving with a side of low-fat Greek yogurt.

5. Optional tip: Feel free to include other vegetables like bell peppers, cucumbers, or roasted sweet potatoes for a more layered dish.

Nutritional Information per Serving

- Calories: 320 kcal
- Total Fat: 9 g (with avocado, varies by size)
- Saturated Fat: 1.5 g
- Cholesterol: 0 mg
- Sodium: 200 mg (varies with added salt and type of beans used)
- Total Carbohydrates: 49 g
- Dietary Fiber: 13 g
- Sugars: 3 g
- Protein: 14 g

Almond Butter and Banana Smoothie

Sometimes, you might not feel like eating anything too heavy or filling in the morning, and that's fine. But it's still important that you get your share of essential nutrients and minerals. The easiest and most convenient way to do that would be to consume them in smoothie form! This particular smoothie recipe doesn't just deliver you with protein, potassium, and healthy fats. It's also so incredibly delicious that you might be tempted to have it every single morning!

Serving Size

- 1

Preparation Time

- 5 minutes

Cooking Time

- No cooking required

Ingredients

- 1 ripe banana
- 1 tablespoon unsweetened and unsalted almond butter
- 1/2 cup low-fat Greek yogurt
- 1/2 cup unsweetened almond milk (or preferred low-fat milk alternative)
- cinnamon to taste
- Ice cubes (optional, for a colder smoothie)

Instructions

1. In a blender, combine the ripe banana, almond butter, low-fat Greek yogurt, and unsweetened almond milk.
2. Add a pinch of cinnamon for extra flavor, if desired.
3. Blend on high until smooth. For a colder smoothie, add a few ice cubes to the blender and blend until smooth.
4. Pour the smoothie into a glass and serve while it is cold.
5. Optional tip: for a sweeter smoothie, feel free to add pitted dates or vanilla extract before blending.

Nutritional Information per Serving

- Calories: 300 kcal

- Total Fat: 10 g
- Saturated Fat: 1 g
- Cholesterol: 5 mg
- Sodium: 100 mg
- Total Carbohydrates: 36 g
- Dietary Fiber: 5 g
- Sugars: 20 g
- Protein: 18 g

Sweet Potato and Spinach Breakfast Hash

Kickstart your day with a nutrient-packed Sweet Potato and Spinach breakfast hash. The fiber from the sweet potato paired with the iron, Vitamin C, and Vitamin E of the spinach, and the protein from the eggs make this dish a perfect balance of healthy and filling, marking the start of a great and productive day.

Serving Size

- 4

Preparation Time

- 15 minutes

Cooking Time

- 20 minutes

Ingredients

- 2 large sweet potatoes, peeled and diced
- 1 tablespoon olive oil

- 1 onion, diced
- 1 red bell pepper, diced
- 2 cups fresh spinach, roughly chopped
- 4 large eggs
- 1 teaspoon smoked paprika
- salt and pepper to taste
- parsley or cilantro for garnish

Instructions

1. Heat the olive oil in a large skillet over medium heat. Add the diced sweet potatoes and cook for about 10 minutes, stirring occasionally, until they begin to soften.

2. Add the diced onion and red bell pepper to the skillet. Continue cooking for another 5-7 minutes until the vegetables are tender and the sweet potatoes are golden brown.

3. Stir in the chopped spinach and smoked paprika. Cook for an additional 2–3 minutes until the spinach has wilted. Season with a sprinkle of salt and pepper.

4. Make four wells in the hash, crack an egg into each well, cover the skillet with a lid, and let the eggs cook for about 4–5 minutes, or until the whites are set but the yolks are still runny.

5. Remove from heat and garnish with fresh herbs before serving.

6. Optional tip: Add chopped nuts or seeds for a crunchier texture.

Nutritional Information per Serving

- Calories: 250 kcal
- Total Fat: 10 g
- Saturated Fat: 2 g
- Cholesterol: 185 mg
- Sodium: 150 mg

- Total Carbohydrates: 30 g

- Dietary Fiber: 5 g

- Sugars: 7 g

- Protein: 12 g

Savory Vegetable and Quinoa Bowl

A warm and hearty meal to start the day is rarely a bad idea. This savory vegetable and quinoa recipe will have your tastebuds bursting with excitement, and you may be tempted to ask for seconds! It's a protein-rich dish that features a medley of sautéed vegetables and a soft-cooked egg.

Serving Size

- 2

Preparation Time

- 10 minutes

Cooking Time

- 20 minutes

Ingredients

- 1 cup quinoa, rinsed

- 2 cups low-sodium vegetable broth

- 1 tablespoon olive oil

- 1 small onion, diced

- 1 red bell pepper, diced

- 1 zucchini, diced

- 1 cup spinach leaves

- 2 large eggs
- salt and pepper to taste
- chopped parsley for garnish

Instructions

1. In a medium saucepan, bring the vegetable broth to a boil. Add the rinsed quinoa, reduce the heat to low, cover, and simmer for about 15 minutes, or until all the liquid is absorbed and the quinoa is tender.

2. While the quinoa is cooking, heat the olive oil in a large skillet over medium heat. Add the onion, bell pepper, and zucchini. Sauté until the vegetables are just tender, about 5–7 minutes.

3. Stir in the spinach and cook until just wilted. Season with salt and pepper.

4. Divide the cooked quinoa between two bowls. Top each bowl with the sautéed vegetables.

5. In the same skillet, fry or poach the eggs to your desired doneness.

6. Place a cooked egg on top of each bowl of quinoa and vegetables.

7. Garnish with fresh parsley before serving.

Nutritional Information per Serving

- Calories: 380 kcal
- Total Fat: 12 g
- Saturated Fat: 2 g
- Cholesterol: 185 mg
- Sodium: 150 mg
- Total Carbohydrates: 50 g
- Dietary Fiber: 8 g
- Sugars: 5 g

- Protein: 20 g

Spinach and Ricotta Breakfast Wraps

Spinach makes another appearance in this cookbook, and for good reason! You already know that it's filled with loads of vitamins and minerals, but did you also know that it can help boost your body's immune system? This time, we've paired spinach with the mild and creamy texture of ricotta cheese for a filling and satisfying breakfast in one neatly wrapped package.

Serving Size

- 4

Preparation Time

- 10 minutes

Cooking Time

- 10 minutes

Ingredients

- 4 whole-grain tortillas
- 1 tablespoon olive oil
- 4 large eggs, beaten
- 2 cups fresh spinach, roughly chopped
- 1/2 cup ricotta cheese, part-skim
- 1/4 cup diced tomatoes
- salt and pepper to taste
- Optional: 1/4 teaspoon crushed red pepper flakes for extra spice

Instructions

1. Heat the olive oil in a large, non-stick skillet over medium heat.

2. Add the beaten eggs and scramble until they are just set.

3. Stir in the chopped spinach and cook until wilted.

4. Remove the skillet from the heat and gently fold in the ricotta cheese and diced tomatoes. Season with salt, black pepper, and red pepper flakes (if using).

5. Warm the tortillas in the microwave or on another skillet.

6. Divide the egg and spinach mixture evenly among the tortillas, placing it on one side of each tortilla.

7. Fold the tortillas over the filling, then fold in the sides, and roll up tightly to form a wrap before serving.

Nutritional Information per Serving

- Calories: 260 kcal
- Total Fat: 13 g
- Saturated Fat: 4 g
- Cholesterol: 215 mg
- Sodium: 320 mg (can vary depending on the use of salt and type of cheese)
- Total Carbohydrates: 22 g
- Dietary Fiber: 3 g
- Sugars: 2 g
- Protein: 16 g

Chapter 5: Lunch Recipes

For many people, the lunch period offers us a moment to break away from the stresses of a typical work day. It gives us an opportunity to recharge and refuel our bodies, while also giving our brains an opportunity to rest and prepare for the afternoon ahead. During this period, it might be tempting to reach for convenient and easy food options that might not necessarily offer the most nutritional value. Some people might even be tempted to skip lunch altogether. It's worth noting that a nutritious lunch is essential for maintaining healthy energy levels throughout the day and avoiding afternoon slumps. In this chapter, we're going to go over a selection of lunch recipes that all subscribe to essential DASH diet principles. Each of these dishes is designed to nourish your body while still supporting your health and wellness goals.

Mediterranean Chickpea Salad

If there's one particular cuisine that promotes healthy living without compromising flavor or gastronomic satisfaction, it's Mediterranean food. This particular Mediterranean-inspired dish is a good embodiment of the DASH diet's focus on legumes, vegetables, and fats that are good for the heart. This Mediterranean chickpea salad is filled with vibrant colors, making it almost too aesthetically pleasing to eat. It's also relatively simple to prepare and execute, making it a convenient option for anyone who wants a satisfying lunch.

Serving Size

- 2

Preparation Time

- 15 minutes

Cooking Time

- No cooking required

Ingredients

- 1 can (15 oz) low-sodium chickpeas, rinsed and drained

- 1 cup cherry tomatoes, halved
- 1 cucumber, diced
- 1/2 red onion, thinly sliced
- 1/4 cup kalamata olives, pitted and halved
- 1/4 cup crumbled feta cheese (low-fat, optional)
- 2 tablespoons olive oil
- Juice of 1 lemon
- 1 garlic clove, minced
- 1 teaspoon dried oregano
- salt and pepper to taste
- A handful of fresh parsley, chopped

Instructions

1. In a large mixing bowl, combine the chickpeas, cherry tomatoes, cucumber, red onion, kalamata olives, and crumbled feta cheese.
2. In a separate small bowl, whisk together the olive oil, lemon juice, minced garlic, dried oregano, salt, and pepper to create the dressing.
3. Pour the dressing over the salad and toss well to ensure all ingredients are evenly coated.
4. Garnish with chopped, fresh parsley.
5. Let the salad sit for about 10 minutes before serving to allow the flavors to meld together.
6. Optional tip: for a protein boost, consider adding sliced grilled chicken breast or tuna to the salad.

Nutritional Information per Serving

- Calories: 350 kcal

- Total Fat: 18 g

- Saturated Fat: 3 g

- Cholesterol: 10 mg

- Sodium: 300 mg

- Total Carbohydrates: 40 g

- Dietary Fiber: 10 g

- Sugars: 8 g

- Protein: 12 g

Grilled Vegetable and Quinoa Wrap

Quinoa is almost like a cheat code, so you can expect that we'll be using it as an ingredient for many of our recipes. It's a great carb option that still offers a healthy dose of protein. Grilled vegetables are also always a good option for anyone looking to get their daily dose of essential vitamins and minerals. This particular salad wrap is filled with nutrients that still pack a punch when it comes to flavor.

Serving Size

- 2

Preparation Time

- 20 minutes

Cooking Time

- 15 minutes

Ingredients

- 2 whole-grain tortillas

- 1/2 cup cooked quinoa

- 1 zucchini, sliced lengthwise

- 1 bell pepper, seeds removed and sliced into strips
- 1/2 red onion, sliced into rings
- 1 tablespoon olive oil
- 1 avocado, sliced
- 2 tablespoons low-fat Greek yogurt
- Juice of 1 lime
- 1/4 teaspoon smoked paprika
- salt and pepper to taste
- handful of spinach leaves

Instructions

1. Preheat the grill to medium-high heat. Toss the zucchini, bell pepper, and red onion in olive oil, and season with salt and pepper.
2. Grill the vegetables until they're tender and charred, about 3–4 minutes per side.
3. In a separate sauce bowl, mix the Greek yogurt, lime juice, and smoked paprika to create a spread.
4. Warm the whole-grain tortillas on the grill for about 30 seconds on each side.
5. Spread a tablespoon of the Greek yogurt mixture onto each tortilla.
6. Layer the grilled vegetables, cooked quinoa, and avocado slices onto each tortilla. Add fresh spinach leaves on top.
7. To form the wraps, roll up the tortillas tightly, folding in the sides as you roll.
8. Optional tip: feel free to experiment with other vegetables based on preference, such as eggplant, asparagus, or portobello mushrooms.

Nutritional Information per Serving

- Calories: 420 kcal

- Total Fat: 20 g
- Saturated Fat: 3 g
- Cholesterol: 2 mg
- Sodium: 320 mg
- Total Carbohydrates: 52 g
- Dietary Fiber: 12 g
- Sugars: 7 g
- Protein: 14 g

Turkey and Avocado Club Salad

A colorful and filling salad can do wonders for replenishing your energy levels during the lunch break so that you can easily power through a busy afternoon. This particular dish combines the lean protein from turkey breast, healthy fats from avocado, and an abundance of vegetables for your much-needed vitamins and minerals. A deliciously light and tangy vinaigrette dresses all of this. This recipe is another example of a dish that is nutrient-rich without compromising flavor.

Serving Size

- 2

Preparation Time

- 15 minutes

Cooking Time

- No cooking necessary if using pre-cooked turkey breast

Ingredients

For the salad:

- 2 cups mixed salad greens (e.g., romaine, spinach, kale, arugula)

- 6 ounces cooked turkey breast, sliced or shredded
- 1 ripe avocado, sliced
- 1 medium tomato, diced
- 1/4 cucumber, sliced
- 2 slices of cooked bacon, crumbled (optional)
- 1 hard-boiled egg, sliced

For the vinaigrette:

- 2 tablespoons olive oil
- 1 tablespoon apple cider vinegar
- 1 teaspoon Dijon mustard
- 1 teaspoon honey (optional)
- salt and pepper to taste

Instructions

1. In a large salad bowl, arrange the mixed salad greens as the base.
2. Evenly distribute the turkey breast, avocado slices, diced tomato, cucumber slices, crumbled bacon, and sliced hard-boiled egg over the greens.
3. In a small bowl, whisk together the olive oil, apple cider vinegar, Dijon mustard, honey, salt, and pepper until well combined.
4. Drizzle the vinaigrette over the salad just before serving.
5. Gently toss the salad to evenly coat all ingredients with the dressing.
6. Optional tip: For a vegetarian-friendly version, substitute the turkey and bacon with tofu or chickpeas for protein.

Nutritional Information per Serving

- Calories: 400 kcal
- Total Fat: 22 g

- Saturated Fat: 4 g

- Cholesterol: 150 mg

- Sodium: 450 mg

- Total Carbohydrates: 14 g

- Dietary Fiber: 7 g

- Sugars: 4 g

- Protein: 35 g

Lentil Soup With Spinach

What's more comforting than a deliciously prepared warm bowl of soup for lunch, especially when you've had to deal with the stresses of the morning workload? This recipe is a classic take on a lentil soup with the added nutritional kick of spinach. It's a dish that's rich in fiber while also offering plant-based protein and other essential nutrients. On top of that, the dish is beginner-friendly, so you don't need any exemplary culinary skills to execute it to perfection. The satisfying flavors paired with the creamy texture can make this a perfect dish, especially on cooler days.

Serving Size

- 4

Preparation Time

- 10 minutes

Cooking Time

- 30 minutes

Ingredients

- 1 tablespoon olive oil

- 1 onion, chopped

- 2 garlic cloves, minced

- 2 carrots, diced
- 2 celery stalks, diced
- 1 cup dried lentils, rinsed and drained
- 4 cups low-sodium vegetable broth
- 2 cups water
- 1 teaspoon ground cumin
- 1/2 teaspoon smoked paprika
- salt and pepper to taste
- 2 cups fresh spinach leaves
- juice of 1 lemon

Instructions

1. Heat the olive oil in a large pot over medium heat. Add the onion and garlic, and sauté until softened, about 3–4 minutes.
2. Add the carrots and celery to the pot, continuing to sauté for another 5 minutes until the vegetables begin to soften.
3. Stir in the lentils, vegetable broth, water, cumin, smoked paprika, salt, and pepper. Bring the mixture to a boil.
4. Once boiling, reduce the heat to low, cover, and simmer for about 20–25 minutes, or until the lentils are tender.
5. Add the spinach leaves to the pot, stirring until wilted. Then, stir in the lemon juice.
6. Taste and adjust seasoning as needed. Serve while hot.
7. Optional tip: for a thicker soup texture, puree half of the soup with an immersion blender before adding the spinach.

Nutritional Information per Serving

- Calories: 250 kcal

- Total Fat: 4 g

- Saturated Fat: 0.5 g

- Cholesterol: 0 mg

- Sodium: 200 mg (varies with the broth and added salt)

- Total Carbohydrates: 38 g

- Dietary Fiber: 16 g

- Sugars: 5 g

- Protein: 14 g

Roasted Vegetable Pita Pocket

Pita pockets are great. They're incredibly easy to make and just as convenient to store and bring around, ready for whenever you're hungry. All sorts of roasted vegetables neatly nestle in a whole-grain pita, filling the pocket itself. This textured and multi-layered dish is a great way to boost your vegetable intake without overindulging. It's a unique dish that's light in its components but can still be very satisfying to consume. Whether you're eating it at home or on-the-go, this pita pocket is sure to be a staple in your rotation.

Serving Size

- 2

Preparation Time

- 15 minutes (plus 20 minutes for roasting vegetables)

Cooking Time

- 20 minutes

Ingredients

- 1 zucchini, sliced into half-moons

- 1 bell pepper, sliced into strips

- 1 small red onion, sliced into wedges
- 8 cherry tomatoes, halved
- 1 tablespoon olive oil
- 1/2 teaspoon dried oregano
- salt and pepper to taste
- 2 whole-grain pita breads, halved
- 1/4 cup hummus
- A handful of fresh spinach or mixed greens
- 1/4 cup crumbled feta cheese (low-fat, optional)

Instructions

1. Preheat your oven to 425 °F (220 °C) and line it with a baking sheet with parchment paper.
2. In a large bowl, toss the zucchini, bell pepper, red onion, and cherry tomatoes with olive oil, dried oregano, and a dash of salt and pepper until well coated.
3. Spread the vegetables on the prepared baking sheet in a single layer. Roast in the preheated oven for about 20 minutes, or until tender and slightly caramelized, stirring halfway through.
4. Warm the pita breads in the oven during the last 2–3 minutes of roasting the vegetables, or toast them lightly in a toaster.
5. Spread a tablespoon of hummus inside each pita half to assemble the pockets. Fill it with a generous serving of the roasted vegetables.
6. Add a few fresh spinach or mixed greens into each pita pocket and sprinkle with crumbled feta cheese.
7. Serve the pita pockets warm or at room temperature.
8. Optional tip: If you're packing this for lunch to go, keep the hummus and vegetables separate from the pita until ready to eat to prevent sogginess.

Nutritional Information per Serving

- Calories: 320 kcal
- Total Fat: 10 g
- Saturated Fat: 2 g
- Cholesterol: 5 mg
- Sodium: 350 mg
- Total Carbohydrates: 50 g
- Dietary Fiber: 8 g
- Sugars: 10 g
- Protein: 12 g

Curried Chicken Salad Lettuce Wraps

Many dishes these days are characterized by the term "flavor bomb," and this recipe is no exception. It's a refreshing and complex twist on the classic chicken salad that we all know and love. Curry's heat and the satisfying crunch of fresh vegetables, wrapped in crisp lettuce leaves, infuse the dish. This dish is a good balance of savory, spicy, and cool, making for an immensely complex gastronomic experience. It's a low-sodium lunch option that doesn't skimp on flavor.

Serving Size

- 2

Preparation Time

- 10 minutes

Cooking Time

- 20 minutes

Ingredients

For the poached chicken:

- 2 boneless, skinless chicken breasts
- 4 cups of water or low-sodium chicken broth
- 1 bay leaf
- A few peppercorns
- 1 clove of garlic, smashed

For the salad:

- 1/4 cup plain low-fat Greek yogurt
- 1 tablespoon curry powder
- 1 apple, diced
- 1/4 cup red bell pepper, diced
- 1/4 cup raisins or dried cranberries
- 1/4 cup almonds, slivered
- salt and pepper to taste

For serving:

- 6 large lettuce leaves (such as Bibb or butter lettuce)
- fresh cilantro, for garnish (optional)

Instructions

1. Start by poaching the chicken. In a large pot, simmer water or low-sodium chicken broth with a bay leaf, peppercorns, and garlic. Make sure to completely submerge the chicken breasts in the pot. Lower the heat and let the chicken poach for 15–20 minutes until it is thoroughly cooked and tender. Take the chicken out of the liquid and allow it to cool.

2. After cooling, tear the chicken into bite-sized pieces and transfer to a large mixing bowl.

3. Add Greek yogurt and curry powder to the shredded chicken and mix until well coated.

4. Incorporate the chopped apple, red bell pepper, raisins (or dried cranberries), and slivered almonds. Season to taste with salt (optional) and pepper, and stir well.

5. Wash and dry the lettuce leaves. Place a spoonful of the curried chicken salad in the center of each leaf.

6. Fold the lettuce over the filling to form a tight roll. If you like, top with fresh cilantro leaves.

7. Enjoy the lettuce wraps right away, or refrigerate them briefly to enhance the flavor fusion.

Nutritional Information per Serving

- Calories: 320 kcal
- Total Fat: 9 g
- Saturated Fat: 1.5 g
- Cholesterol: 65 mg
- Sodium: 250 mg (adjust based on the use of salt and type of broth)
- Total Carbohydrates: 25 g
- Dietary Fiber: 5 g
- Sugars: 17 g
- Protein: 35 g

Hearty Minestrone Soup

Italian cuisine is beloved all over the world. And with popular dishes that make use of fresh ingredients like whole wheat pasta, tomatoes, bell peppers, lean meats, seafood, cheese, and other healthy food items, it's certainly a cuisine that offers a good value proposition. This particular recipe for a hearty minestrone soup is perfect for people who might subscribe to the DASH diet. It's a wholesome take on a classic dish that's rich in vegetables, beans, and whole grains. There are few things in life that are as warm and comforting as a good bowl of soup.

Serving Size

- 4

Preparation Time

- 15 minutes

Cooking Time

- 40 minutes

Ingredients

- 1 tablespoon olive oil
- 1 onion, diced
- 2 carrots, diced
- 2 stalks of celery, diced
- 3 cloves of garlic, minced
- 1 zucchini, diced
- 1 small yellow squash, diced
- 1 cup chopped green beans
- 1 can (15 oz) low-sodium diced tomatoes, undrained
- 1 can (15 oz) low-sodium kidney beans, rinsed and drained
- 6 cups low-sodium vegetable broth
- 1/2 cup whole wheat pasta (small shapes like shells or macaroni)
- 1 teaspoon dried oregano

- 1 teaspoon dried basil
- salt and pepper to taste
- 1/4 cup freshly grated Parmesan cheese (optional, for serving)
- fresh parsley, chopped (for garnish)

Instructions

1. Heat the olive oil in a large soup pot over medium heat. Add the onion, carrots, and celery, sautéing until the vegetables start to soften, about 5 minutes.
2. Add the garlic, zucchini, yellow squash, and green beans. Cook, stirring occasionally, for another 5 minutes until the vegetables are slightly tender.
3. Stir in the diced tomatoes (with their juice), kidney beans, vegetable broth, dried oregano, and dried basil. Bring the soup to a boil.
4. Once boiling, reduce the heat to a simmer and add the whole wheat pasta. Cook for about 10–15 minutes, or until the pasta is tender.
5. Season the soup to taste with salt and pepper. Let it simmer for a few more minutes for the flavors to meld together.
6. Serve the minestrone hot, garnished with freshly chopped parsley and a sprinkle of Parmesan cheese on top.
7. Optional tip: Customize the soup by adding any seasonal vegetables that you might be fond of.

Nutritional Information per Serving

- Calories: 260 kcal
- Total Fat: 5 g
- Saturated Fat: 1 g
- Cholesterol: 2 mg
- Sodium: 300 mg
- Total Carbohydrates: 45 g

- Dietary Fiber: 10 g
- Sugars: 8 g
- Protein: 12 g

Tuna and White Bean Salad

Fish might be one of the healthiest forms of protein that you could incorporate into your diet. Tuna, in particular, is rich in Omega-3 fatty acids, which translates to good heart health. In addition to that, tuna is a healthy source of lean protein without the unhealthy fats, making it a good low-calorie protein. This delicious dish pairs tuna with white beans for some added fiber to aid in the digestive process. Crisp vegetables and a zesty lemon dressing further enhance the entire recipe. It's a no-fuss meal that offers a ton of flavor with plenty of nutrients.

Serving Size

- 2

Preparation Time

- 10 minutes

Cooking Time

- No cooking required

Ingredients

- 1 can (5 oz) low-sodium white tuna in water, drained and flaked
- 1 can (15 oz) low-sodium white beans, rinsed and drained
- 1/2 red onion, finely sliced
- 1/2 cucumber, diced
- 1/2 cup cherry tomatoes, halved
- 2 tablespoons chopped fresh parsley
- 2 tablespoons olive oil

- juice of 1 lemon
- 1 garlic clove, minced
- salt and pepper to taste
- mixed greens or arugula for serving

Instructions

1. In a large mixing bowl, combine the flaked tuna, white beans, red onion, cucumber, cherry tomatoes, and chopped parsley.
2. In a small bowl, whisk together the olive oil, lemon juice, minced garlic, and a pinch of salt and pepper until well incorporated. This will serve as your dressing.
3. Pour the dressing over the tuna and bean mixture. Gently toss to ensure the dressing coats all ingredients evenly.
4. To serve, place a generous bed of mixed greens or arugula, on each plate. Place the tuna and white bean salad on top.
5. Optional tip: For an extra touch of freshness and flavor, add a final squeeze of lemon juice to each serving.

Nutritional Information per Serving

- Calories: 350 kcal
- Total Fat: 10 g
- Saturated Fat: 1.5 g
- Cholesterol: 30 mg
- Sodium: 400 mg
- Total Carbohydrates: 35 g
- Dietary Fiber: 8 g
- Sugars: 3 g
- Protein: 25 g

Sweet Potato and Black Bean Burritos

When you think of low-sodium and heart-healthy foods, you might not necessarily think of tacos or burritos. But that doesn't necessarily have to be the case. Of course, you're going to have to do a little bit of tweaking, but don't worry. This recipe still has a ton of flavor without violating the rules of the DASH diet. It's a vegetarian burrito that's rich in fiber and protein with an array of spices for a multi-layered gastronomic experience.

Serving Size

- 4

Preparation Time

- 20 minutes

Cooking Time

- 25 minutes

Ingredients

- 2 medium sweet potatoes, peeled and diced
- 1 tablespoon olive oil
- 1 teaspoon ground cumin
- 1/2 teaspoon smoked paprika
- salt and pepper to taste
- 1 can (15 oz) low-sodium black beans, rinsed and drained
- 1/2 red onion, finely chopped
- 1 garlic clove, minced
- juice of 1 lime
- 4 whole-grain tortillas
- 1/2 cup fresh cilantro, chopped

- 1 avocado, sliced
- 1/4 cup low-fat sour cream or Greek yogurt (optional)
- 1/4 cup shredded low-fat cheese (optional)

Instructions

1. Preheat the oven to 425 °F (220 °C). Toss the diced sweet potatoes with olive oil, cumin, smoked paprika, and a pinch of salt and pepper until well seasoned.

2. Spread the potatoes across a baking sheet and roast in the oven for about 20–25 minutes, or until tender and slightly caramelized.

3. While the sweet potatoes are roasting, heat a small amount of olive oil in a pan over medium heat. Sauté the red onion and garlic until soft and fragrant, or about 5 minutes. Continue cooking the black beans and lime juice until they reach the desired level of heat.

4. Warm the whole-grain tortillas in the oven for a few minutes or on a dry pan over medium heat for about 30 seconds on each side.

5. To assemble the burritos, lay out each tortilla on a flat surface. Divide the roasted sweet potato, black bean mixture, cilantro, avocado slices, and a dollop of sour cream or Greek yogurt among the tortillas. Sprinkle with shredded cheese.

6. Fold in the sides of each tortilla and roll up tightly to enclose the filling.

7. Serve immediately, with extra lime wedges on the side for squeezing.

8. Optional tip: Make your own low-sodium salsa to pair with your burritos.

Nutritional Information per Serving

- Calories: 400 kcal
- Total Fat: 12 g
- Saturated Fat: 2 g
- Cholesterol: 5 mg
- Sodium: 300 mg

- Total Carbohydrates: 62 g
- Dietary Fiber: 15 g
- Sugars: 8 g
- Protein: 14 g

Mediterranean Quinoa Salad Bowl

Surprise, surprise! Quinoa makes another appearance on our list of DASH-friendly recipes and that shouldn't be a surprise. This time, we're combining fluffy quinoa with a bounty of fresh vegetables, chickpeas, and a zesty lemon-olive oil dressing. Consider this dish to be a celebration of different textures and flavors. You'll feel so full after this meal that you won't feel tempted to eat anything else until dinnertime.

Serving Size

- 2

Preparation Time

- 15 minutes

Cooking Time

- 20 minutes

Ingredients

- 1 cup quinoa, rinsed
- 2 cups water or low-sodium vegetable broth
- 1 cup chickpeas, rinsed and drained (low-sodium canned)
- 1 cucumber, diced
- 1 bell pepper, diced
- 1/2 cup cherry tomatoes, halved
- 1/4 cup red onion, finely chopped

- 1/4 cup Kalamata olives, pitted and halved
- 1/4 cup crumbled feta cheese (low-fat)
- 2 tablespoons chopped fresh parsley

For the dressing:

- 3 tablespoons olive oil
- Juice of 1 lemon
- 1 garlic clove, minced
- 1 teaspoon dried oregano
- salt and pepper to taste

Instructions

1. In a medium saucepan, bring two cups of water or vegetable broth to a boil.
2. Stir in the quinoa, then reduce the heat to low, cover, and simmer for 15–20 minutes, or until the liquid is absorbed and the quinoa is fluffy.
3. In a large bowl, mix the cooked quinoa with chickpeas, cucumber, bell pepper, cherry tomatoes, red onion, Kalamata olives, and crumbled feta cheese.
4. For the dressing, combine olive oil, lemon juice, minced garlic, dried oregano, and a pinch of salt and pepper in a small bowl, whisking until well blended.
5. Drizzle the dressing over the quinoa mixture and toss to coat everything evenly. Top the salad with chopped fresh parsley before serving.
6. Enjoy the salad either at room temperature or chilled, according to your liking.

Nutritional Information per Serving

- Calories: 450 kcal
- Total Fat: 20 g
- Saturated Fat: 4 g
- Cholesterol: 15 mg

- Sodium: 300 mg
- Total Carbohydrates: 52 g
- Dietary Fiber: 10 g
- Sugars: 8 g
- Protein: 16 g

Lemon Herb Tuna Salad

Revitalize your lunch with the Lemon Herb Tuna Salad, a dish that's both light and packed with flavor. This salad blends flaky tuna, fresh vegetables, and a tangy lemon herb dressing, offering a meal that's not just low in sodium but also abundant in omega-3 fatty acids and fiber. It's a superb option for those seeking a swift, wholesome meal that's simple to make and ideal for an active lifestyle.

Serving Size

- 4

Preparation Time

- 10 minutes

Ingredients

- 2 cans (5 oz each) low-sodium tuna in water, drained
- 1 cup cherry tomatoes, halved
- 1 cucumber, diced
- 1 red bell pepper, diced
- 1/4 cup red onion, finely chopped
- 1/4 cup fresh parsley, chopped
- 2 tablespoons fresh basil, chopped

- 2 tablespoons olive oil
- juice of 1 lemon
- mixed salad greens
- salt and pepper to taste

Instructions

1. Combine the drained tuna, cherry tomatoes, cucumber, red bell pepper, and red onion in a large mixing bowl.
2. In a separate small bowl, whisk together the olive oil, lemon juice, chopped parsley, and basil to create the dressing. Add salt and pepper, if you wish.
3. Pour the dressing over the tuna and vegetable mixture and toss gently to coat everything evenly.
4. Let the salad sit for about 5 minutes to allow the flavors to meld together.
5. Serve the tuna salad over a bed of mixed salad greens.

Nutritional Information per Serving

- Calories: 180 kcal
- Total Fat: 7 g
- Saturated Fat: 1 g
- Cholesterol: 30 mg
- Sodium: 150 mg
- Total Carbohydrates: 8 g
- Dietary Fiber: 2 g
- Sugars: 4 g
- Protein: 20 g

Asian Chicken Salad With Sesame Ginger

Dressing

Add a dash of sunshine to your lunch meal with this delicious recipe for an Asian-inspired chicken salad. This vibrant and tangy dish features a fusion of flavors for your palate that's sure to ignite your senses. You get a nutritious blend of lean protein from the chicken, as well as vitamins and minerals from the vegetables. Antioxidants are also abundant in the salad's ginger dressing.

Serving Size

- 4

Preparation Time

- 20 minutes

Cooking Time

- 10 minutes

Ingredients

- 2 chicken breasts
- 2 cups cabbage, shredded
- 1 carrot, julienned
- 1 red bell pepper, thinly sliced
- 1/2 cup snap peas, trimmed
- 1/4 cup green onions, sliced
- 1/4 cup cilantro, chopped
- 2 tablespoons sesame seeds, toasted

For the dressing:

- 3 tablespoons sesame oil
- 2 tablespoons soy sauce (low sodium)

- 1 tablespoon rice vinegar
- 1 tablespoon honey
- 1 teaspoon fresh ginger, grated
- 1 garlic clove, minced

Instructions

1. Cook the chicken breast in a pan over medium heat until cooked through, approximately 10 minutes. Let cool after cooking.
2. Once cooled, tear the chicken breast apart into shredded strips and set aside.
3. In a large mixing bowl, combine the shredded cabbage, julienned carrot, sliced red bell pepper, trimmed snap peas, green onions, and chopped cilantro.
4. In a smaller bowl, whisk together the sesame oil, soy sauce, rice vinegar, honey, grated ginger, and minced garlic to create the dressing.
5. Pour the dressing over the vegetable mixture and toss well to coat.
6. Add the shredded chicken to the salad and gently stir until everything is well combined.
7. Sprinkle toasted sesame seeds over the top of the salad.
8. Serve the salad immediately, or chill it in the refrigerator for about 30 minutes before serving for enhanced flavors.

Nutritional Information per Serving

- Calories: 280 kcal
- Total Fat: 14 g
- Saturated Fat: 2 g
- Cholesterol: 60 mg
- Sodium: 200 mg
- Total Carbohydrates: 12 g

- Dietary Fiber: 3 g

- Sugars: 6 g

- Protein: 25 g

Smoky BBQ Tempeh Wrap

Lunches don't have to be boring, and this smoky barbecue tempeh wrap is proof of that! It's a dish that's just bursting at the seams with all sorts of bold flavors and diverse textures. The recipe offers a low-sodium BBQ sauce that makes it perfect for those who are on the DASH diet and watching their sodium levels.

Serving Size

- 4

Preparation Time

- 15 minutes

Cooking Time

- 10 minutes

Ingredients

- 8 oz tempeh, sliced into thin strips

- 1 tablespoon olive oil

- 1/2 cup low-sodium BBQ sauce

- 4 whole-grain tortillas

- 1 cup shredded lettuce

- 1 carrot, julienned

- 1 red bell pepper, julienned

- 1/4 red onion, thinly sliced

- Spanish paprika to taste

Instructions

1. Heat the olive oil in a skillet over medium heat. Add the tempeh strips and sauté until they start to brown, about 5 minutes.

2. Coat the tempeh strips with the low-sodium BBQ sauce, turning them frequently, until they are well-coated and thoroughly heated, which should take about another 5 minutes. Sprinkle with paprika according to taste.

3. Warm the whole-grain tortillas in a microwave or on a skillet to make them pliable.

4. To assemble the wraps, lay each tortilla flat and distribute the shredded lettuce, julienned carrot, bell pepper, and red onion evenly among the tortillas.

5. Place the BBQ tempeh strips down the center of each tortilla.

6. Roll up the tortillas tightly, tucking in the edges to hold the filling in.

7. Cut each wrap in half diagonally and serve immediately.

Nutritional Information per Serving

- Calories: 300 kcal
- Total Fat: 9 g
- Saturated Fat: 2 g
- Cholesterol: 0 mg
- Sodium: 300 mg
- Total Carbohydrates: 40 g
- Dietary Fiber: 6 g
- Sugars: 12 g
- Protein: 16 g

Chickpea Curry Sandwich

Curry is perhaps one of India's greatest gifts to the world of cuisine, with its rich and inviting flavor that always leaves you wanting just a little bit more. This recipe for a chickpea curry sandwich provides a substantial amount of fiber and protein to have you feeling full and satisfied all throughout the afternoon. The sandwich combines a hearty whole-grain bread with a creamy, slightly spicy chickpea salad.

Serving Size

- 4

Preparation Time

- 15 minutes

Ingredients

- 1 can (15 oz) chickpeas, rinsed and drained
- 1/4 cup low-fat Greek yogurt
- 1 tablespoon curry powder
- 1 apple, diced
- 1 celery stalk, diced
- 1/4 cup raisins
- 1/4 cup chopped walnuts
- salt and pepper to taste
- 8 slices whole-grain bread
- lettuce leaves

Instructions

1. In a large bowl, mash the chickpeas with a fork or potato masher until coarsely mashed, leaving some texture.

2. Add the Greek yogurt and curry powder to the mashed chickpeas, mixing until well combined.

3. Stir in the diced apple, diced celery, raisins, and chopped walnuts. Season with salt and pepper, to taste.

4. Lay out four slices of whole-grain bread. Place a few lettuce leaves on each slice.

5. Spoon the curried chickpea salad evenly onto the lettuce-covered bread slices. Top each with another slice of bread to form sandwiches.

6. Cut each sandwich in half before serving.

Nutritional Information per Serving

- Calories: 350 kcal

- Total Fat: 9 g

- Saturated Fat: 1 g

- Cholesterol: 1 mg

- Sodium: 300 mg

- Total Carbohydrates: 55 g

- Dietary Fiber: 10 g

- Sugars: 15 g

- Protein: 15 g

Chapter 6:
Dinner Recipes

After a long day of arduous tasks and mundane errands, it's nice to go home and unwind with a fresh and hearty meal. Ideally, you want these recipes to be easy to execute so that you won't have to stress too much over what to prepare after a tiring day. But you don't want to put so little effort into your meals to the point that they're not satisfying. The recipes that we'll use in this chapter are relatively easy to prepare and are full of flavor and texture. You'll never feel like you're cheating yourself with any of the meals here, as you're sure to be left feeling satiated and satisfied. Remember, the key to sustaining any kind of DIET is learning how to fall in love with the process. If preparing and eating these meals feels like a chore or a duty, then staying on track becomes a lot more difficult. But if you find a simple and efficient way to create meals that taste great, then it won't even feel like dieting at all!

Lemon-Herb Baked Salmon With Asparagus

End your day on a high note with this Lemon-Herb Baked Salmon with Asparagus. It's a heavy dish that offers a lot of heart-healthy omega-3 fatty acids. Don't forget all the nutrient-rich goodness that comes with the asparagus, either! All of this comes together so well with the light citrus-herb dressing that will feel like a summer party in your mouth. It's a simple and elegant dinner that's a feast for the eyes, mouth, and body.

Serving Size

- 2

Preparation Time

- 10 minutes

Cooking Time

- 20 minutes

Ingredients

- 2 salmon fillets (about 6 ounces each)
- 1 bunch asparagus, ends trimmed

- 2 tablespoons olive oil
- 1 lemon, thinly sliced
- 2 teaspoons fresh dill, chopped (or 1 teaspoon dried dill)
- 2 garlic cloves, minced
- salt and pepper to taste

Instructions

1. Preheat your oven to 400°F (200°C). For an easy cleanup, line a baking sheet with parchment paper.
2. On one side of this sheet, lay out the asparagus in a single layer. Drizzle them with 1 tablespoon of olive oil, then season with salt and pepper to taste. Toss them to ensure they're well coated.
3. On the opposite side, place the salmon fillets. Brush each one with the remaining olive oil and season with salt and pepper.
4. Top the salmon with minced garlic and dill, then arrange lemon slices over and around the fish and asparagus.
5. Bake everything in your preheated oven for 15-20 minutes, or until the salmon is flaky and the asparagus is tender yet crisp.
6. Garnish the dish with fresh dill and serve hot.
7. Optional tip: The dish also pairs well with a side of quinoa for some added protein and fiber.

Nutritional Information per Serving

- Calories: Approximately 350 kcal
- Total Fat: 22 g
- Saturated Fat: 3 g
- Cholesterol: 75 mg
- Sodium: 100 mg (adjust based on salt usage)

- Total Carbohydrates: 8 g
- Dietary Fiber: 3 g
- Sugars: 2 g
- Protein: 30 g

Stuffed Bell Peppers With Quinoa and Black Beans

Many people judge bell peppers unfairly. But it's an incredibly versatile spice that adds so much color and flavor to any meal. And for this particular dish, we're going to allow the bell peppers to serve as the vessels for our ever-reliable quinoa and black beans. We're going to stuff our bell peppers with a healthy mix of quinoa, black beans, and vegetables, along with a sprinkle of low-fat cheese for some added flavor and texture. It's a fantastic way to enjoy a variety of nutrients from plant-based sources in a relatively simple but beautiful package.

Serving Size

- 4

Preparation Time

- 15 minutes

Cooking Time

- 35 minutes

Ingredients

- 4 large bell peppers, any color, tops cut off, and seeds removed
- 1 cup cooked quinoa
- 1 can (15 oz) low-sodium black beans, rinsed and drained
- 1 cup corn kernels (fresh, canned, or thawed from frozen)
- 1/2 cup diced tomatoes (fresh or canned without added salt)

- 1/2 cup red onion, finely chopped
- 2 cloves garlic, minced
- 1 teaspoon ground cumin
- 1/2 teaspoon chili powder
- 1/4 cup fresh cilantro, chopped
- juice of 1 lime (or lemon)
- 1/2 cup shredded low-fat cheese
- salt and pepper to taste

Instructions

1. Preheat the oven to 375 °F (190 °C). Lightly grease a baking dish with olive oil.
2. In a large bowl, mix together the cooked quinoa, black beans, corn, diced tomatoes, red onion, garlic, cumin, chili powder, cilantro, and lime juice. Season with salt and pepper, to taste.
3. Stuff each bell pepper with the quinoa mixture, packing it in tightly. Place the stuffed peppers upright in the prepared baking dish, making sure that it won't topple over.
4. Cover the dish with aluminum foil and bake in the preheated oven for about 25–30 minutes, or until the peppers are tender.
5. Remove the foil, top each pepper with shredded cheese, and return to the oven. Continue baking for an extra 5 minutes, ensuring the cheese melts and becomes bubbly.
6. Serve the stuffed peppers hot, garnished with additional chopped cilantro.
7. Optional tip: Add ground turkey or chicken cooked with the same spices for some extra protein.

Nutritional Information per Serving

- Calories: 280 kcal
- Total Fat: 5 g

- Saturated Fat: 1 g
- Cholesterol: 5 mg
- Sodium: 200 mg
- Total Carbohydrates: 48 g
- Dietary Fiber: 10 g
- Sugars: 8 g
- Protein: 14 g

Herb-Crusted Chicken and Roasted Vegetables

There's a rustic charm that accompanies this herb-crusted chicken dish that's just so incredibly hard to resist. It's a protein-rich meal that still satisfies the basic principles of the DASH diet. The dish features a succulent chicken breast as the star of the show. A blend of aromatic herbs encrusts the versatile protein, while a medley of seasonally fresh vegetables complements it. You can't get any simpler than that. And yet, despite its simplicity, the elegance of this understated dish cannot be overstated.

Serving Size

- 4

Preparation Time

- 15 minutes

Cooking Time

- 30 minutes

Ingredients

- 4 boneless, skinless chicken breasts
- 2 tablespoons olive oil, divided
- 1 teaspoon dried rosemary

- 1 teaspoon dried thyme
- 1/2 teaspoon garlic powder
- 2 cups small new potatoes, halved
- 1 cup carrots, sliced
- 1 cup green beans, trimmed
- 1 red bell pepper, cut into chunks
- 1 onion, cut into wedges
- salt and pepper to taste

Instructions

1. Preheat the oven to 425 °F (220 °C). Line a large baking sheet with parchment paper.
2. In a small bowl, mix together the rosemary, thyme, garlic powder, salt, and pepper. Rub each chicken breast with a bit of olive oil and coat generously with the herb mixture.
3. Arrange the chicken breasts in the center of the prepared baking sheet.
4. In a large bowl, toss the potatoes, carrots, green beans, bell pepper, and onion with the remaining olive oil and a sprinkle of salt and pepper. On a baking sheet, scatter the vegetables around the chicken.
5. Bake the chicken in the preheated oven for approximately 25–30 minutes, or until it reaches an internal temperature of 165 °F or 74 °C, and the vegetables become tender and caramelized.
6. Serve the herb-crusted chicken warm, surrounded by the roasted vegetables.
7. Optional tip: Marinate the chicken breasts with the herb and olive oil mixture for a few hours in the fridge for a more pronounced flavor.

Nutritional Information per Serving

- Calories: 350 kcal
- Total Fat: 10 g

- Saturated Fat: 1.5 g
- Cholesterol: 75 mg
- Sodium: 200 mg (adjust based on the use of salt)
- Total Carbohydrates: 30 g
- Dietary Fiber: 5 g
- Sugars: 5 g
- Protein: 35 g

Balsamic Glazed Pork Chops With Roasted Sweet Potatoes

Although the health and fitness community often demonizes pork, this is not always the case. When cooked properly, pork can be a healthy source of lean protein. So, even if you're on the DASH diet, which prioritizes food that's friendly toward blood pressure levels, you don't necessarily have to give up pork entirely. This particular dish is able to capitalize on the savory richness of the pork and pairs it with the caramel-like flavor of the starchy sweet potatoes. You can even make a large batch in one go for multiple servings that you can return to throughout the week!

Serving Size

- 4

Preparation Time

- 15 minutes

Cooking Time

- 25 minutes

Ingredients

- 4 boneless pork chops, about 1-inch thick

- 2 tablespoons olive oil, divided
- 2 medium sweet potatoes, peeled and cut into 1-inch cubes
- 1/4 cup balsamic vinegar
- 2 teaspoons honey
- 1 teaspoon fresh rosemary, finely chopped
- 1 garlic clove, minced
- salt and pepper to taste

Instructions

1. Preheat your oven to 425 °F (220 °C) and line a baking sheet with parchment paper. Coat the sweet potato cubes with 1 tablespoon of olive oil and a pinch of salt and pepper, then spread them on the sheet. Roast for 20–25 minutes until they're tender and slightly caramelized, stirring once halfway through.

2. As the sweet potatoes roast, warm the remaining olive oil in a large skillet over medium-high heat. Season both sides of the pork chops with salt and pepper.

3. Place the pork chops in the skillet and cook for 4–5 minutes per side, or until the internal temperature reaches 145 °F (63 °C). Remove them from the skillet and let them rest.

4. In the same skillet, combine balsamic vinegar, honey, rosemary, and minced garlic over low heat. Stir until the mixture becomes a thick glaze, which should take about 2–3 minutes.

5. Pour the balsamic glaze over the pork chops and serve with the roasted sweet potatoes.

Nutritional Information per Serving

- Calories: 400 kcal
- Total Fat: 14 g
- Saturated Fat: 3 g
- Cholesterol: 90 mg

- Sodium: 150 mg (adjust based on the use of salt)
- Total Carbohydrates: 35 g
- Dietary Fiber: 5 g
- Sugars: 12 g
- Protein: 35 g

Beef and Broccoli Stir-Fry

We're shifting gears once more with this dish as we move toward Asia with this oriental-inspired beef and broccoli dish. The recipe calls for the robust flavors of tender beef, paired with the crunch and freshness of broccoli. A savory sauce then envelops all of this, adhering to the low-sodium principles of the DASH diet. You won't have to worry about this dish lacking in flavor and you can rest assured that you're not skimping on nutrition either.

Serving Size

- 4

Preparation Time

- 15 minutes

Cooking Time

- 10 minutes

Ingredients

- 1 lb (450g) lean beef (such as flank steak), thinly sliced against the grain
- 4 cups broccoli florets
- 2 tablespoons olive oil, divided
- 2 garlic cloves, minced

For the sauce:

- 1/4 cup low-sodium soy sauce
- 2 tablespoons water
- 1 tablespoon cornstarch
- 1 tablespoon honey
- 1 teaspoon fresh ginger, grated
- 1/2 teaspoon chili flakes (optional)

Instructions

1. In a small bowl, combine low-sodium soy sauce, water, cornstarch, honey, grated ginger, and chili flakes (optional) to prepare the sauce. Set this mixture aside.

2. Then, heat one tablespoon of olive oil in a large skillet or wok over medium-high heat. Sauté the garlic until it becomes fragrant, which should take about 30 seconds.

3. Place the beef in the skillet in a single layer and let it sear undisturbed for 1–2 minutes. Proceed to stir-fry the beef until it is almost fully cooked, approximately 2–3 minutes, then remove it from the skillet.

4. Using the same skillet, add another tablespoon of olive oil and the broccoli florets. Stir-fry the broccoli until it turns bright green and is tender yet crisp, about 3–4 minutes.

5. Reintroduce the beef to the skillet with the broccoli, pour the previously prepared sauce over it, and mix well. Continue to cook for an additional 1–2 minutes until the sauce thickens and coats the ingredients evenly.

6. Finally, season with salt and pepper according to your preference.

7. Optional tip: Pair the dish with a cup of brown rice or quinoa for some healthy carbohydrates.

Nutritional Information per Serving

- Calories: 300 kcal
- Total Fat: 10 g

- Saturated Fat: 2 g
- Cholesterol: 60 mg
- Sodium: 350 mg
- Total Carbohydrates: 20 g
- Dietary Fiber: 3 g
- Sugars: 6 g
- Protein: 30 g

Spicy Garlic Shrimp With Quinoa

Shrimps might be a little high in cholesterol, especially when compared to other proteins, but it can still be a very good source of lean protein when consumed in moderation. Again, the whole point of the DASH diet is that it isn't restrictive eating. You can still enjoy good dishes without feeling guilty. We're going to pair shrimp with our beloved quinoa for added protein and fiber while keeping sodium in check. To enhance the flavor of this dish, we'll make use of garlic and chili to spice things up without compromising nutrition.

Serving Size

- 4

Preparation Time

- 10 minutes

Cooking Time

- 20 minutes

Ingredients

- 1 cup quinoa, rinsed
- 2 cups low-sodium vegetable broth
- 1 lb (450g) shrimp, peeled and deveined

- 2 tablespoons olive oil, divided
- 3 garlic cloves, minced
- 1/2 teaspoon red pepper flakes (adjust to taste)
- juice of 1 lemon
- 1 tablespoon fresh parsley, chopped
- Salt (optional) and pepper to taste
- 1 bell pepper, diced
- 1 cup cherry tomatoes, halved
- 1 zucchini, diced

Instructions

1. Cook the quinoa according to the package instructions. Once cooked, fluff with a fork and set aside.

2. While the quinoa is cooking, heat 1 tablespoon of olive oil in a large skillet over medium-high heat. Add the shrimp, minced garlic, red pepper flakes, salt, and pepper. Sauté the shrimp until they are pink and cooked through, or about 3–4 minutes. Remove the shrimp from the skillet and set aside.

3. In the same skillet, add the remaining tablespoon of olive oil. Sauté the diced bell pepper, cherry tomatoes, and zucchini until they start to soften, about 5–7 minutes.

4. Return the shrimp to the skillet with the vegetables, add the lemon juice, and stir to combine. Cook for an additional 1–2 minutes to reheat the shrimp and blend the flavors.

5. Before serving, serve the shrimp over the cooked quinoa and garnish with fresh parsley.

6. Optional tip: Cook the quinoa with low-sodium vegetable broth for added flavor.

Nutritional Information per Serving

- Calories: 350 kcal

- Total Fat: 10 g
- Saturated Fat: 1.5 g
- Cholesterol: 180 mg
- Sodium: 250 mg (adjust based on the use of salt and broth)
- Total Carbohydrates: 35 g
- Dietary Fiber: 5 g
- Sugars: 3 g
- Protein: 28 g

Rosemary and Dijon Mustard Baked Chicken

Chicken breasts are known by many to be one of the best sources of lean protein. However, it has also garnered a reputation for being a relatively bland and boring protein. But that's certainly not the case if you know how to prepare and season your chicken breast properly! With this recipe, we're going to infuse this meaty poultry with the deep aromatic essence of rosemary and the tangy kick of Dijon mustard. By the time the first bite of chicken reaches your lips, you'll realize that this chicken dish is far from boring or bland. This recipe is a perfect complement for a variety of sides.

Serving Size

- 4

Preparation Time

- 10 minutes

Cooking Time

- 25 minutes

Ingredients

- 4 boneless, skinless chicken breasts

- 2 tablespoons Dijon mustard
- 2 tablespoons olive oil
- 2 garlic cloves, minced
- 2 teaspoons fresh rosemary, finely chopped (or 1 teaspoon dried rosemary)
- salt and pepper to taste
- lemon wedges as garnish for serving

Instructions

1. Preheat the oven to 375 °F (190 °C). Line a baking sheet with parchment paper.
2. In a small bowl, mix the Dijon mustard, olive oil, minced garlic, rosemary, and a pinch of salt and pepper until well-seasoned.
3. Place the chicken breasts on the prepared baking sheet. Brush the mustard mixture evenly over both sides of each chicken breast.
4. Bake the chicken in the preheated oven for about 20 to 25 minutes, or until the internal temperature reaches 165 °F (74 °C) and the outside is slightly golden.
5. Let the chicken rest for a few minutes before slicing. Serve with lemon wedges on the side for added zest.

Nutritional Information per Serving

- Calories: 220 kcal
- Total Fat: 8 g
- Saturated Fat: 1 g
- Cholesterol: 75 mg
- Sodium: 200 mg (varies based on the use of salt and type of mustard)
- Total Carbohydrates: 1 g
- Dietary Fiber: 0 g
- Sugars: 0 g

- Protein: 34 g

Maple-Glazed Salmon With Steamed Broccoli

If you're a fan of sweet and savory dishes, then you are surely going to be delighted by this delicious maple-glazed salmon recipe. Salmon is a great protein because of the nutritional values that it offers, but it's also an immensely versatile meat. There are so many ways you can prepare it and this particular recipe capitalizes on that. Paired with the salmon is a nutrient-packed broccoli that adds color and texture to the dish.

Serving Size

- 4

Preparation Time

- 10 minutes

Cooking Time

- 15 minutes

Ingredients

- 4 salmon fillets (about 6 ounces each)
- 1 tablespoon olive oil
- 1/4 cup pure maple syrup
- 2 tablespoons low-sodium soy sauce
- 1 garlic clove, minced
- 1 teaspoon fresh ginger, grated
- 4 cups broccoli florets
- salt and pepper to taste
- lemon wedges as garnish for serving

Instructions

1. Preheat your oven to 400 °F (200 °C). Line a baking sheet with parchment paper or lightly grease it with olive oil.

2. Place the salmon fillets on the prepared baking sheet. Brush each fillet with olive oil and season lightly with salt and pepper.

3. In a small bowl, whisk together the maple syrup, low-sodium soy sauce, minced garlic, and grated ginger. Pour half of this mixture over the salmon fillets, reserving the rest for serving.

4. Bake the salmon in the preheated oven for about 12–15 minutes, or until the salmon flakes easily with a fork.

5. While the salmon is baking, steam the broccoli florets until tender-crisp, about 5–7 minutes.

6. Serve the maple-glazed salmon with the steamed broccoli on the side. Drizzle the remaining maple-soy mixture over the salmon right before serving together with the lemon wedges.

7. Optional tip: For an extra crispy salmon crust, broil the protein for the final 1–2 minutes of cooking.

Nutritional Information per Serving

- Calories: 350 kcal
- Total Fat: 14 g
- Saturated Fat: 2 g
- Cholesterol: 75 mg
- Sodium: 300 mg
- Total Carbohydrates: 18 g
- Dietary Fiber: 3 g
- Sugars: 12 g
- Protein: 34 g

Grilled Lamb Chops With Mint Yogurt Sauce

Lamb might not necessarily be a popular protein for many because of its strong gamy flavor, but when prepared well, it can be the star of any dinner table. This particular recipe lets the natural flavors of the lamb chops shine while complementing it with a refreshing and light mint yogurt sauce to offset the richness of the meat. This recipe offers you a substantial amount of protein without any unwanted fats that could violate the principles of the DASH diet.

Serving Size

- 4

Preparation Time

- 15 minutes (without marinating time)

Cooking Time

- 10 minutes

Ingredients

- 8 lamb chops
- 2 tablespoons olive oil
- 2 garlic cloves, minced
- 1 teaspoon dried rosemary
- salt and pepper to taste

For the mint yogurt sauce:

- 1 cup low-fat Greek yogurt
- 1/4 cup fresh mint leaves, finely chopped
- 1 tablespoon lemon juice
- 1 garlic clove, minced

- salt and pepper to taste

Instructions

1. In a small bowl, mix together olive oil, minced garlic, dried rosemary, salt, and pepper. Rub this mixture all over the lamb chops. Cover and let the chops marinate in the refrigerator for at least 1 hour, or overnight for deeper flavor.

2. Preheat the grill to medium-high heat. Grill the lamb chops for 3–5 minutes on each side for medium-rare, or until they reach your desired level of doneness.

3. While the lamb is grilling, prepare the Mint Yogurt Sauce by combining Greek yogurt, chopped mint, lemon juice, minced garlic. Season lightly with salt and pepper. Stir until well mixed.

4. Serve the lamb chops with a drizzle of mint yogurt sauce on top or on the side.

5. Optional tip: Prepare the mint yogurt sauce ahead of time and refrigerate it to allow the flavors to meld.

Nutritional Information per Serving

- Calories: 400 kcal
- Total Fat: 25 g
- Saturated Fat: 9 g
- Cholesterol: 105 mg
- Sodium: 200 mg (varies based on the use of salt)
- Total Carbohydrates: 4 g
- Dietary Fiber: 0 g
- Sugars: 2 g
- Protein: 38 g

Tangy Baked Cod With Capers

Fish is always a good idea when you're looking to get your fill of healthy fats and lean proteins. This recipe drifts away from usual fish like tuna and salmon by making use of cod, a light and natural-tasting fish that works well with all sorts of spices and marinades. In this dish, we're going to make use of lemons and capers to really accentuate the freshness of the fish. At the end of the day, when you're on the DASH diet, you can never go wrong with lightly seasoned fish and vegetables for any meal.

Serving Size

- 4

Preparation Time

- 10 minutes

Cooking Time

- 15 minutes

Ingredients

- 4 cod fillets (about 6 ounces each)
- 2 tablespoons olive oil
- juice and zest of 1 lemon
- 2 tablespoons capers, rinsed
- 2 garlic cloves, minced
- 1 teaspoon dried parsley (or 1 tablespoon fresh parsley, chopped)
- salt and pepper to taste
- additional lemon wedges for garnish

Instructions

1. Preheat your oven to 400°F (200°C). Line a baking sheet with parchment paper or lightly grease it.

2. Place the cod fillets on the prepared baking sheet. Drizzle each fillet with olive oil and squeeze lemon juice evenly over them.

3. Sprinkle the lemon zest, capers, minced garlic, and parsley over the cod. Season with a pinch of salt and pepper.

4. Bake in the preheated oven for about 12–15 minutes, or until the cod is opaque and flakes easily with a fork.

5. Serve the baked cod with lemon wedges as garnish.

Nutritional Information per Serving

- Calories: 200 kcal
- Total Fat: 7 g
- Saturated Fat: 1 g
- Cholesterol: 60 mg
- Sodium: 250 mg (varies based on the use of salt and capers)
- Total Carbohydrates: 2 g
- Dietary Fiber: 0 g
- Sugars: 0 g
- Protein: 30 g

Garlic and Lemon Roasted Chicken

Savor the homely comfort and nourishment of this simple and rustic chicken dish. This recipe showcases chicken thighs steeped in a mixture of fresh herbs, garlic, and lemon, yielding meat that is tender within and crunchy without. Paired with an assortment of roasted vegetables, it offers a single-pan meal that's easy to prepare without compromising flavor or nutritional value.

Serving Size

- 4

Preparation Time

- 15 minutes

Cooking Time

- 40 minutes

Ingredients

- 8 bone-in, skin-on chicken thighs
- 2 tablespoons olive oil
- Juice and zest of 1 lemon
- 3 garlic cloves, minced
- 1 teaspoon dried rosemary
- 1 teaspoon dried thyme
- 1/2 teaspoon dried oregano
- salt and pepper to taste
- lemon wedges for serving

Instructions

1. Preheat the oven to 375 °F (190 °C). Line a baking sheet with parchment paper.
2. In a small bowl, mix together the olive oil, lemon juice and zest, minced garlic, rosemary, thyme, oregano, salt, and pepper. Mix well to create the marinade.
3. Place the chicken thighs in a large bowl or resealable plastic bag. Pour the marinade over the chicken, ensuring each piece is well coated. If time allows, let the chicken marinate in the refrigerator for at least 30 minutes, or up to 4 hours.
4. Arrange the marinated chicken thighs on the prepared baking sheet. Roast in the preheated oven for about 35–40 minutes, or until the chicken is golden brown, crispy, and cooked through (internal temperature reaches 165°F or 74 °C).
5. Serve the roasted chicken thighs hot, garnished with additional fresh herbs, if desired, and lemon wedges on the side.
6. Optional tip: Marinade the chicken for a longer time to fully allow the flavors to incorporate into the meat.

Nutritional Information per Serving

- Calories: 450 kcal
- Total Fat: 28 g
- Saturated Fat: 6 g
- Cholesterol: 185 mg
- Sodium: 300 mg (adjust based on the use of salt)
- Total Carbohydrates: 1 g
- Dietary Fiber: 0 g
- Sugars: 0 g
- Protein: 35 g

Seared Scallops With Citrus Quinoa Salad

Scallops are ocean treasures, and this dish perfectly captures the creamy and sweet flavors of this beloved seafood. It's a light and satisfying dish that fits perfectly within the diet plan of a DASH subscriber. This recipe pairs succulent seared scallops with a vibrant, citrus-infused quinoa salad, offering a perfect balance of protein, whole grains, and antioxidants. It's an ideal choice for a nutritious dinner that's both simple and elegant.

Serving Size

- 4

Preparation Time

- 15 minutes

Cooking Time

- 10 minutes

Ingredients

- 12 large sea scallops, patted dry
- 1 tablespoon olive oil
- 1 cup quinoa, rinsed
- 2 cups low-sodium vegetable broth
- 1 orange, zest and juice
- 1 lemon, zest and juice
- 1/2 cup chopped fresh parsley
- 1/4 cup sliced almonds, toasted
- 1/4 cup dried cranberries
- 2 tablespoons chopped fresh mint
- salt and pepper to taste

Instructions

1. Cook the quinoa in the vegetable broth according to package instructions. Once cooked, fluff with a fork and set aside to cool slightly.

2. In a large bowl, combine the cooked quinoa with the orange zest, orange juice, lemon zest, lemon juice, parsley, almonds, cranberries, and mint. Toss thoroughly to combine, and season with salt (if using) and pepper. Set aside.

3. Heat the olive oil in a large skillet over medium-high heat. Lightly season the scallops with salt and pepper. Once the oil is shimmering, add the scallops to the pan without overcrowding.

4. Cook the scallops for about 2 minutes per side, or until they have a golden crust and are just cooked through.

5. To serve, divide the citrus quinoa salad among plates and top with the seared scallops.

6. Garnish with additional parsley or mint, if desired.

Nutritional Information per Serving

- Calories: 350 kcal
- Total Fat: 9 g
- Saturated Fat: 1 g
- Cholesterol: 30 mg
- Sodium: 200 mg
- Total Carbohydrates: 45 g
- Dietary Fiber: 6 g
- Sugars: 10 g
- Protein: 20 g

Veal Piccata With Steamed Broccoli

Veal is another example of a lean meat that you can occasionally indulge in while on the DASH diet. This recipe features tender veal escalopes lightly pan-fried and then finished with a vibrant lemon-caper sauce, providing a burst of flavor in each bite. Served with steamed broccoli, this dish is low in sodium, high in protein, and full of nutrients, making it a healthy and tasty option for dinner.

Serving Size

- 4

Preparation Time

- 15 minutes

Cooking Time

- 20 minutes

Ingredients

- 4 veal escalopes (about 4 oz each)

- 1/4 cup all-purpose flour (for dusting)
- 2 tablespoons olive oil
- 1/3 cup low-sodium chicken broth
- Juice of 1 lemon
- 2 tablespoons capers, rinsed
- 2 tablespoons fresh parsley, chopped
- 1 large head of broccoli, cut into florets
- salt and pepper to taste

Instructions

1. Season the flour with a little salt and pepper. Lightly dust each veal with flour and shake off any excess.
2. Heat the olive oil in a large skillet over medium-high heat. When hot, add the veal and cook for about 2–3 minutes on each side or until golden and cooked through. Remove the veal from the skillet and set aside on a warm plate.
3. In the same skillet, add the chicken broth and lemon juice, scraping up any brown bits from the pan. Bring to a simmer and let reduce slightly, about 3 minutes.
4. Add the capers and half of the parsley, and stir to combine. Return the veal to the skillet and coat with the sauce. Cook for another 1–2 minutes to ensure the veal is heated through and coated with the sauce.
5. While making the sauce, steam the broccoli until just tender, about 4–5 minutes.
6. Serve the veal escalopes with the steamed broccoli on the side. Drizzle any remaining sauce over the veal, then garnish with the remaining parsley.

Nutritional Information per Serving

- Calories: 300 kcal
- Total Fat: 12 g
- Saturated Fat: 2 g

- Cholesterol: 90 mg
- Sodium: 200 mg
- Total Carbohydrates: 10 g
- Dietary Fiber: 3 g
- Sugars: 2 g
- Protein: 35 g

DASH-Friendly Sloppy Joe

Forget about the sloppy Joes you used to eat as a kid in your school cafeteria. This recipe for sloppy joe is much more wholesome in terms of nutritional value, and you'll certainly appreciate the melding together of the flavors of its natural ingredients. It's a tasty, heart-healthy alternative to traditional beef sloppy joes, packed with more nutrients and less sodium.

Serving Size

- 4

Preparation Time

- 10 minutes

Cooking Time

- 20 minutes

Ingredients

- 1 tablespoon olive oil
- 1 lb ground turkey (93% lean)
- 1 onion, finely chopped
- 1 red bell pepper, diced

- 2 cloves garlic, minced
- 1 zucchini, diced
- 1 cup low-sodium tomato sauce
- 2 tablespoons tomato paste
- 1 tablespoon Worcestershire sauce (ensure it's low sodium)
- 1 tablespoon apple cider vinegar
- 1 tablespoon brown sugar or honey
- salt and pepper to taste
- 4 whole-grain hamburger buns

Instructions

1. Warm the olive oil in a large skillet over medium heat. Cook the ground turkey in the skillet, crumbling it with a spoon, until browned and fully cooked, about 5–7 minutes.

2. Incorporate the onion, red bell pepper, and garlic into the skillet with the turkey. Continue to cook, stirring occasionally, until the vegetables have softened, which will take around 5 minutes.

3. Mix in the diced zucchini and let it cook for an additional 3–4 minutes, until it's slightly tender.

4. In the skillet, pour the tomato sauce, tomato paste, Worcestershire sauce, apple cider vinegar, and either brown sugar or honey. Stir thoroughly to blend all the components.

5. Reduce the heat to low and let the mixture simmer for approximately 10 minutes, or until it thickens to your liking. Season with salt (optional) and pepper.

6. Optionally, toast the whole-grain buns until they are lightly crisp.

7. Heap the turkey and vegetable mixture onto the bottom halves of the buns, then cap them with the top halves.

Nutritional Information per Serving

- Calories: 350 kcal
- Total Fat: 12 g
- Saturated Fat: 3 g
- Cholesterol: 70 mg
- Sodium: 300 mg
- Total Carbohydrates: 35 g
- Dietary Fiber: 5 g
- Sugars: 10 g
- Protein: 28 g

Chapter 7: Snacks and Desserts

Embracing the DASH diet doesn't necessarily mean that you have to deprive yourself of the pleasures of having delicious and comforting desserts or snacks. In fact, with the richness of the recipes that we've gone through so far, no one would blame you for wanting to cleanse your palate with something sweet and slightly sinful. Snacking is also normal, especially if you're an active person who lives a fast-paced lifestyle. You need those extra calories to help power you through the day. In this chapter, we'll cover some simple snacks and desserts that you can enjoy without having to feel guilty about it. Again, the DASH diet isn't about deprivation. Establishing a healthy relationship with food is crucial to ensuring your body receives the necessary nourishment.

Cinnamon Apple Chips

The first dish that we'll discuss in this chapter works effectively as both a snack and a dessert. The sweet aroma of the cinnamon apple chips will have you salivating, eager to take bite after bite as you savor that addicting crunch. We bake these apple chips to perfection, making them DASH-friendly. So, you don't have to worry about the unhealthy byproducts of deep-frying traditional potato chips. Whether you're packing these as snacks on-the-go or if you want to enjoy it as a post-dinner treat, either way, you're sure to be satisfied. This recipe is proof that it's possible to enjoy snacks or desserts guiltlessly!

Serving Size

- 4

Preparation Time

- 10 minutes

Cooking Time

- 2 hours

Ingredients

- 4 large apples (preferably a sweet variety)

- 1 teaspoon ground cinnamon

Instructions

1. Preheat your oven to 200 °F (93 °C). Line two baking sheets with parchment paper.

2. Core the apples and slice them very thinly, aiming for consistent thickness to ensure even baking.

3. Arrange the apple slices in a single layer on the prepared baking sheets. Sprinkle the slices evenly with ground cinnamon.

4. Bake in the preheated oven for 1 hour. Then, flip the apple slices over and continue baking for another hour, or until the slices are dry and crisp. Monitor them closely to avoid burning, given that oven temperatures can fluctuate.

5. Let the apple chips cool completely on the baking sheets. They will continue to crisp up as they cool.

6. Serve the cinnamon apple chips as a crunchy, sweet snack.

7. Store any leftovers in an airtight container.

8. Optional tip: For an extra hint of sweetness, add a light sprinkle of stevia or a drizzle of honey.

Nutritional Information per Serving

- Calories: 95 kcal
- Total Fat: 0 g
- Saturated Fat: 0 g
- Cholesterol: 0 mg
- Sodium: 0 mg
- Total Carbohydrates: 25 g
- Dietary Fiber: 4 g
- Sugars: 19 g (natural sugars from apples)

- Protein: 0 g

Greek Yogurt Parfait

Think of Greek yogurt as a life hack for when you're craving a healthy version of ice cream! Of course, Greek yogurt isn't naturally sweet, and that's why we're going to supplement its flavor with a healthy heap of mixed berries along with the nutty notes of crunchy granola. This dessert isn't just one that caters to people who have a sweet tooth. It's a perfectly acceptable snack or dessert for people who religiously follow the DASH diet. This parfait is the embodiment of creating something that is both nourishing and satisfying at the same time. Feel free to enjoy this luxurious dish after a meal or as a snack in between your bigger meals!

*** Serving Size ***

- 4

*** Preparation Time ***

- 10 minutes

*** Cooking Time ***

- No cooking required

*** Ingredients ***

- 2 cups low-fat Greek yogurt
- 2 cups mixed berries (such as strawberries, blueberries, raspberries, and blackberries)
- 1 cup low-sodium granola
- 1 tablespoon honey or maple syrup (optional)
- fresh mint leaves for garnish (optional)

Instructions

1. Begin by layering 1/4 cup of Greek yogurt at the bottom of four glasses or parfait jars.

2. Add a layer of mixed berries over the yogurt in each glass.

3. Sprinkle a generous tablespoon of granola over the berries.

4. Continue layering the yogurt, berries, and granola until the glasses are completely filled.

5. Drizzle a little honey or maple syrup over the top layer for added sweetness, if desired.

6. Garnish each parfait with fresh mint leaves for a refreshing touch.

7. Refrigerate for up to an hour before serving to allow the flavors to meld together.

8. Optional tip: Choose a granola that's low in sugar and sodium to maintain the healthiness of the parfait.

Nutritional Information per Serving

- Calories: Calories: 220 kcal
- Total Fat: 3 g
- Saturated Fat: 1 g
- Cholesterol: 10 mg
- Sodium: 65 mg
- Total Carbohydrates: 36 g
- Dietary Fiber: 4 g
- Sugars: 22 g (includes natural sugars from fruits and optional sweeteners
- Protein: 15 g

Savory Roasted Chickpeas

The small and humble chickpea might look insignificant, but you would be surprised at how satisfying and filling it can be, especially when cooked the right way. For this recipe, our humble chickpeas will be seasoned with a blend of spices and roasted to absolute perfection. The satisfying crisp of the roasted chickpeas, together with the complex spices, will have you craving a bag whenever you find yourself feeling hungry in the middle of the afternoon. They also work great as toppings for soups or salads!

Serving Size

- 4

Preparation Time

- 5 minutes

Cooking Time

- 20 to 25 minutes

Ingredients

- 2 cans (15 oz each) low-sodium chickpeas, rinsed and drained
- 2 tablespoons olive oil
- 1/2 teaspoon smoked paprika
- 1/2 teaspoon garlic powder
- 1/4 teaspoon cayenne pepper (adjust to taste)
- salt and pepper to taste

Instructions

1. Preheat your oven to 400 °F (200 °C). Line a baking sheet with parchment paper.
2. Dry the chickpeas thoroughly with paper towels or a clean kitchen towel. Removing as much moisture as possible will help them crisp up in the oven.

3. In a bowl, toss the chickpeas with olive oil, smoked paprika, garlic powder, cayenne pepper, and a pinch of salt (if using) and pepper until evenly coated.

4. Spread the chickpeas in a single layer on the prepared baking sheet.

5. Roast in the preheated oven for 20 to 25 minutes, or until golden brown and crispy, shaking the pan or stirring the chickpeas halfway through to ensure even cooking.

6. Let the chickpeas cool slightly and crisp up before serving.

Nutritional Information per Serving

- Calories: 180 kcal
- Total Fat: 8 g
- Saturated Fat: 1 g
- Cholesterol: 0 mg
- Sodium: 200 mg (varies based on the use of salt)
- Total Carbohydrates: 20 g
- Dietary Fiber: 6 g
- Sugars: 0 g
- Protein: 6 g

Dark Chocolate and Almond Energy Bites

Who says that chocolate has to be unhealthy? Well, we're not exactly eating Snickers or Reese's Peanut Butter Cup here, but at least we can get pretty close to that level of satisfaction without having to sacrifice our health! This recipe offers you a guilt-free way to indulge in the rich flavors of dark chocolate while also benefiting from its antioxidant properties. Don't forget the nutritional boost that comes with the almonds and oats, either! This is a great light snack that you can have for a quick energy boost before a workout.

Serving Size

- Makes about 12 bites

Preparation Time

- 15 minutes (plus chilling time)

Cooking Time

- No cooking required

Ingredients

- 1 cup rolled oats
- 1/2 cup almond butter
- 1/4 cup dark chocolate chips (at least 70% cocoa)
- 1/4 cup honey or maple syrup
- 1/4 cup ground flaxseed
- 2 tablespoons chopped almonds
- 1 teaspoon vanilla extract
- pinch of salt

Instructions

1. In a large mixing bowl, combine the rolled oats, almond butter, dark chocolate chips, honey (or maple syrup), ground flaxseed, chopped almonds, vanilla extract, and a pinch of salt. Stir until the mixture is well combined and sticky.

2. Using clean hands or a cookie scoop, form the mixture into small balls, about 1 inch in diameter. If the mixture is too sticky, refrigerate it for 10–15 minutes before forming the balls.

3. Place the formed energy bites on a baking sheet lined with parchment paper. Refrigerate for at least 30 minutes to set.

4. Once set, transfer the energy bites to an airtight container and store in the refrigerator. Serve chilled.

Nutritional Information per Serving (1 bite)

- Calories: 120 kcal
- Total Fat: 7 g
- Saturated Fat: 1.5 g
- Cholesterol: 0 mg
- Sodium: 20 mg
- Total Carbohydrates: 12 g
- Dietary Fiber: 2 g
- Sugars: 7 g
- Protein: 3 g

Spiced Roasted Pumpkin Seeds

Don't underestimate the power of pumpkin seeds! These tiny treasures are proof that big things do indeed come in small packages. Protein, magnesium, zinc, and a variety of other minerals are abundant in pumpkin seeds. It's exactly the kind of snack that you can feel good about indulging in. This particular recipe elevates the humble pumpkin seed into a gourmet snack that's as delicious as it is nutritious. The combination of smoked paprika, garlic, and cayenne pepper flavors with the seeds results in a bolder and more complex taste.

Serving Size

- 4

Preparation Time

- 10 minutes

Cooking Time

- 20 minutes

Ingredients

- 1 cup raw pumpkin seeds, cleaned and patted dry
- 1 tablespoon olive oil
- 1/2 teaspoon smoked paprika
- 1/4 teaspoon garlic powder
- 1/4 teaspoon onion powder
- cayenne pepper to taste
- salt and pepper to taste

Instructions

1. Preheat your oven to 350 °F (175 °C). Line a baking sheet with parchment paper.
2. Coat the pumpkin seeds evenly with olive oil in a bowl. Add the smoked paprika, garlic powder, onion powder, cayenne pepper, and a pinch of salt and black pepper. Stir until the seeds are well coated with the spices.
3. Spread the pumpkin seeds in a single layer on the prepared baking sheet.
4. Roast in the preheated oven for about 20 minutes, or until the seeds are golden and crispy. Stir halfway through to ensure even roasting.
5. Let the pumpkin seeds cool on the baking sheet before serving. They will continue to crisp up as they cool.

Nutritional Information per Serving

- Calories: 180 kcal
- Total Fat: 15 g
- Saturated Fat: 2.5 g

- Cholesterol: 0 mg
- Sodium: 5 mg
- Total Carbohydrates: 3 g
- Dietary Fiber: 1 g
- Sugars: 0 g
- Protein: 9 g

No-Bake Peanut Butter Energy Balls

Peanut butter is a great snack in itself, especially if it's the natural, unsweetened variety. It is incredibly filling and rich in healthy fats, carbohydrates, and proteins. That's why it also makes for a great ingredient when developing more complex dishes without having to resort to other unhealthy ingredients. This delightful treat is sure to satisfy your sweet tooth while also providing you with essential nutrients. And you don't even need any baking skills to perfect this insanely delicious and filling snack.

Serving Size

- Makes about 12 balls.

Preparation Time

- 15 minutes (plus chilling time)

Cooking Time

- No cooking required

Ingredients

- 1 cup rolled oats
- 1/2 cup natural peanut butter
- 1/3 cup honey or agave syrup
- 1/2 cup ground flaxseed

- 1/2 cup unsweetened dark chocolate chips (optional)
- 1 teaspoon vanilla extract
- pinch of salt

Instructions

1. In a large mixing bowl, combine the rolled oats, natural peanut butter, honey (or agave syrup), ground flaxseed, dark chocolate chips, vanilla extract, and a pinch of salt. Mix the ingredients thoroughly until the mixture holds together.
2. Using clean hands, roll the mixture into small balls, about 1-inch in diameter. If the mixture is too sticky, refrigerate it for 10–15 minutes before rolling.
3. To set, place the formed balls on a parchment paper-lined baking sheet and refrigerate for at least 30 minutes.
4. Once set, transfer the energy balls to an airtight container and allow to cool in refrigerator prior to serving.

Nutritional Information per Serving

- Calories: 150 kcal
- Total Fat: 8 g
- Saturated Fat: 1 g
- Cholesterol: 0 mg
- Sodium: 50 mg
- Total Carbohydrates: 18 g
- Dietary Fiber: 3 g
- Sugars: 10 g
- Protein: 4 g

Almond Oatmeal Cookies

Cookies don't always have to be sinful. Indulge in a healthier dessert option with these Almond Oatmeal Cookies, packed with loads of fiber and no artificial sweeteners. These cookies take the heart-healthy benefits of oats and combine them with the natural sweetness that comes from applesauce and honey. It's not only a delicious treat to have in-between meals or as a dessert, but also a great source of protein and fiber.

Serving Size

- 12 cookies (approx.)

Preparation Time

- 15 minutes

Cooking Time

- 15 minutes

Ingredients

- 1 cup rolled oats

- 3/4 cup whole wheat flour

- 1/2 teaspoon baking soda

- 1/4 teaspoon salt (optional)

- 1 teaspoon cinnamon

- 1/2 cup unsweetened applesauce

- 1/4 cup honey (or maple syrup for a vegan option)

- 1/4 cup unsweetened almond milk

- 1 teaspoon vanilla extract

- 1/2 cup almonds, chopped

- 1/4 cup raisins (optional)

Instructions

1. Preheat your oven to 350 °F (175 °C) and line a baking sheet with parchment paper.

2. Combine rolled oats, whole wheat flour, baking soda, salt, and cinnamon in a large bowl.

3. In a separate bowl, whisk applesauce, honey, almond milk, and vanilla extract until well blended.

4. Mix the wet ingredients into the dry ingredients until just combined, then fold in the chopped almonds and raisins.

5. Ensure that you space the tablespoon-sized dollops of dough about 2 inches apart on the lined baking sheet.

6. Bake in the preheated oven for approximately 15 minutes, or until the cookies are golden brown around the edges and set in the center.

7. After baking, allow the cookies to cool on the sheet for 5 minutes before transferring them to a wire rack to cool completely.

8. Optional tip: Customize the cookies by adding other ingredients like dried cranberries, dark chocolate chips, or flax seeds for additional flavor and nutrients.

Nutritional Information per Serving

- Calories: 120 kcal
- Total Fat: 4 g
- Saturated Fat: 0.5 g
- Cholesterol: 0 mg
- Sodium: 75 mg (varies depending on the use of salt)
- Total Carbohydrates: 18 g
- Dietary Fiber: 2 g
- Sugars: 8 g

- Protein: 3 g

Avocado and Hummus Veggie Sandwich

The Avocado and Hummus Veggie Sandwich is a delightful, light snack that effectively quells mid-day hunger because of the dish's healthy fats and fiber content. Brimming with the creamy texture of avocado and the savory taste of hummus, this sandwich is packed with vegetables, offering both an interesting crunchy texture and a wealth of nutrients. It's a convenient source of fiber, healthy fats, and plant-based protein for those who are looking for more amino acids while sticking to a vegetarian lifestyle.

Serving Size

- 2

Preparation Time

- 10 minutes

Ingredients

- 4 slices whole-grain bread
- 1/2 ripe avocado, sliced
- 4 tablespoons hummus
- 1 small cucumber, thinly sliced
- 1 small carrot, grated
- 1/2 red bell pepper, thinly sliced
- red onion slices
- handful of fresh spinach leaves
- salt and pepper to taste

Instructions

1. Begin by lightly toasting the slices of whole-grain bread to enhance their crunchiness and keep them from becoming soggy.

2. Apply one tablespoon of hummus to each slice.

3. On two slices, arrange layers of avocado, cucumber, grated carrot, red bell pepper, red onion, and spinach leaves.

4. Season with a pinch of salt and pepper.

5. Place the other slices of bread on top, hummus side facing inward, and press down gently to bind the ingredients.

6. Slice each sandwich diagonally into halves before serving.

7. Optional tip: For added protein, consider adding a few slices of turkey or chicken breast.

Nutritional Information per Serving

- Calories: 350 kcal
- Total Fat: 14 g
- Saturated Fat: 2 g
- Cholesterol: 0 mg
- Sodium: 300 mg (varies depending on the use of salt and type of hummus)
- Total Carbohydrates: 45 g
- Dietary Fiber: 12 g
- Sugars: 8 g
- Protein: 12 g

Coconut Chia Pudding

This pudding blends the exotic taste of coconut with the nutritional benefits of chia seeds, resulting in a dessert rich in omega-3 fatty acids, fiber, and plant protein. It's a simple delight that firms up in the refrigerator, ideal for an anytime snack without guilt. You would be hard-pressed to find any dessert that's as healthy, easy to prepare, and delicious as this.

Serving Size

- 4

Preparation Time

- 10 minutes

Ingredients

- 1/4 cup chia seeds
- 1 cup coconut milk (light, for fewer calories)
- 1 cup unsweetened almond milk
- 2 tablespoons honey or maple syrup (adjust to taste)
- 1 teaspoon vanilla extract
- Optional toppings: sliced fresh fruits, berries, toasted coconut flakes, or nuts

Instructions

1. In a mixing bowl, combine the chia seeds, coconut milk, almond milk, honey (or maple syrup), and vanilla extract. Whisk together until well blended.
2. Divide the mixture evenly among four dessert cups or small jars.
3. Cover and refrigerate for at least 4 hours, preferably overnight, until the pudding has thickened, and the chia seeds have fully expanded.
4. Once the pudding has set, stir it to distribute the seeds evenly. If the pudding is too thick, adjust the consistency by adding a little more almond milk and mixing well.
5. Serve chilled, topped with your choice of fresh fruits, berries, toasted coconut flakes, or nuts for added texture and flavor.

Nutritional Information per Serving

- Calories: 180 kcal

- Total Fat: 9 g
- Saturated Fat: 3 g
- Cholesterol: 0 mg
- Sodium: 50 mg
- Total Carbohydrates: 23 g
- Dietary Fiber: 5 g
- Sugars: 12 g (includes natural and added sugars)
- Protein: 3 g

Chapter 8: Vegetable Dishes

One major point that we're reiterating over and over again throughout this cookbook is that the DASH diet is not restrictive. In fact, it's the opposite of that. Despite the DASH diet's primary focus on blood pressure regulation and heart health promotion, its flexibility allows it to accommodate individuals with diverse health and wellness goals or philosophies. It's a common misconception that following the DASH diet can be restrictive and that being a vegetarian only exacerbates that problem. But that certainly isn't the case.

Vegetable dishes can be immensely effective in terms of their nutritional value and versatility. In this chapter, we're going to showcase to you how it's possible to have a wide array of vegetable dishes that will expand your gastronomic exposure and experiences.

Roasted Brussels Sprouts With Balsamic Glaze

Brussels sprouts frequently get a bad rap, especially with people who may not be fond of eating vegetables at all. But this often-misunderstood vegetable can certainly shine as the star of a dish when cooked and seasoned properly. In this recipe, you'll get to experience the caramelized and crispy delight of a roasted Brussels sprout along with the tangy reduction of balsamic vinegar. After eating this, you'll see Brussels sprouts in a completely new light.

Serving Size

- 4

Preparation Time

- 10 minutes

Cooking Time

- 25 minutes

Ingredients

- 1 lb (about 450g) Brussels sprouts, trimmed and halved

- 2 tablespoons olive oil
- 1/4 cup balsamic vinegar
- 2 tablespoons honey or maple syrup
- salt and pepper to taste

Instructions

1. Preheat your oven to 400 °F (200 °C). Line a baking sheet with parchment paper.
2. In a large bowl, toss the Brussels sprouts with olive oil and season with salt and black pepper until evenly coated.
3. Spread the Brussels sprouts in a single layer on the prepared baking sheet, cut side down.
4. Roast in the preheated oven for about 20–25 minutes, or until they are golden brown and crispy on the edges.
5. While the Brussels sprouts are roasting, prepare the balsamic glaze. In a small saucepan, bring the balsamic vinegar and honey (or maple syrup) to a simmer over medium heat. Reduce the mixture by half, stirring occasionally, until it thickens into a syrup-like consistency, about 10 minutes.
6. Drizzle the balsamic glaze over the roasted Brussels sprouts immediately after removing them from the oven.
7. Optional tip: Add a sprinkle of grated Parmesan cheese or a handful of chopped nuts (like walnuts or almonds) to the Brussels sprouts before roasting for some added flavor.

Nutritional Information per Serving

- Calories: 160 kcal
- Total Fat: 7 g
- Saturated Fat: 1 g
- Cholesterol: 0 mg
- Sodium: 30 mg (varies based on the use of salt)

- Total Carbohydrates: 23 g
- Dietary Fiber: 4 g
- Sugars: 12 g
- Protein: 3 g

Grilled Vegetable Quinoa Salad

Quinoa makes another appearance in this cookbook, and why not? People often accuse vegetarians of not consuming enough protein, but this isn't always the case. In fact, food items like quinoa are perfect for people who want to stick to vegetarian diets because of how much protein they pack. In this recipe, we celebrate the diversity and power of plant-based ingredients. There's beauty in simplicity, and this dish embodies that phrase so poignantly.

Serving Size

- 4

Preparation Time

- 20 minutes

Cooking Time

- 30 minutes

Ingredients

- 1 cup quinoa, rinsed
- 2 cups water or low-sodium vegetable broth
- 1 zucchini, sliced lengthwise
- 1 yellow squash, sliced lengthwise
- 1 red bell pepper, seeded and quartered
- 1 eggplant, sliced into rounds

- 2 tablespoons olive oil
- salt and pepper to taste

For the dressing:

- 1/4 cup olive oil
- Juice and zest of 1 lemon
- 2 garlic cloves, minced
- 1 tablespoon fresh parsley, finely chopped
- 1 tablespoon fresh basil, finely chopped
- salt and pepper to taste

Instructions

1. In a medium saucepan, bring 2 cups of water or vegetable broth to a boil. Reduce the heat to low, cover, and simmer the quinoa for about 15–20 minutes, or until it absorbs all the liquid. Fluff with a fork and set aside to cool.
2. Preheat your grill to medium-high heat. Brush the zucchini, yellow squash, bell pepper, and eggplant with olive oil and season lightly with some salt and pepper.
3. Grill the vegetables, turning occasionally, for about 10 minutes until they are tender and charred. Remove from the grill and let them cool slightly. Then, chop the vegetables into bite-sized pieces.
4. In a small bowl, whisk together the ingredients for the lemon-herb dressing.
5. In a large bowl, combine the cooled quinoa and grilled vegetables. Pour the lemon-herb dressing over the salad and toss to combine.
6. Serve the salad at room temperature or chilled, depending on your preference.
7. Optional tip: To add more protein to the dish, consider incorporating chickpeas or black beans into the mix!

Nutritional Information per Serving

- Calories: 350 kcal

- Total Fat: 18 g
- Saturated Fat: 2.5 g
- Cholesterol: 0 mg
- Sodium: 100 mg
- Total Carbohydrates: 42 g
- Dietary Fiber: 8 g
- Sugars: 6 g
- Protein: 8 g

Eggplant and Chickpea Curry

This simple eggplant and chickpea curry recipe is a hearty and comforting dish that so elegantly showcases the gastronomic prowess of plant-based ingredients. It expertly combines the distinct texture of eggplants with the nutty taste of chickpeas, all drenched in a spicy and savory curry sauce.

Serving Size

- 4

Preparation Time

- 15 minutes

Cooking Time

- 30 minutes

Ingredients

- 2 tablespoons olive oil
- 1 large onion, finely chopped
- 2 garlic cloves, minced

- 1 tablespoon fresh ginger, grated
- 1 large eggplant, cut into 1-inch cubes
- 1 can (15 oz) chickpeas, rinsed and drained
- 1 can (14 oz) diced tomatoes, no salt added
- 1 can (14 oz) coconut milk, light
- 2 teaspoons curry powder
- 1 teaspoon ground cumin
- 1/2 teaspoon turmeric
- 1/2 teaspoon chili powder (adjust to taste)
- salt and pepper to taste
- fresh cilantro, chopped for garnish

Instructions

1. Heat the olive oil in a large skillet or saucepan over medium heat. Add the onion, garlic, and ginger, cooking until the onion is translucent and fragrant, about 5 minutes.

2. Add the eggplant cubes to the skillet, stirring to coat with the onion mixture. Cook until the eggplant starts to soften, about 8 minutes.

3. Stir in the chickpeas, diced tomatoes, coconut milk, curry powder, ground cumin, turmeric, and chili powder. Bring the mixture to a simmer, then reduce the heat and cover. Let it cook for about 15–20 minutes, or until the eggplant is tender and the flavors have melded together.

4. Season the curry with salt and pepper, to taste. If the curry is too thick, add a little water or additional coconut milk to reach your desired consistency.

5. Serve the curry together with naan bread, rice, quinoa, or your preferred side.

Nutritional Information per Serving

- Calories 350 kcal

- Total Fat: 12 g

- Saturated Fat: 5 g

- Cholesterol: 0 mg

- Sodium: 300 mg

- Total Carbohydrates: 50 g

- Dietary Fiber: 13 g

- Sugars: 13 g

- Protein: 12 g

Portobello Mushroom Steaks With Herb Sauce

Who says that only meat eaters can enjoy steaks? Vegetarians can also enjoy the savory and rich flavors of a well-seasoned steak, albeit in the form of a mushroom. Rich and smoky flavors infuse this specific dish, perfectly complementing a vibrant and herbaceous sauce. No one will blame you for wanting to indulge in these mushroom steaks two, three, or even four times a week. They're just that good. Oh, and don't forget the fact that mushrooms are nutrient-rich and safe for those who are trying to maintain a strict diet!

Serving Size

- 4

Preparation Time

- 15 minutes

Cooking Time

- 20 minutes

Ingredients

- 4 large portobello mushrooms, stems removed

- 2 tablespoons olive oil

- 2 tablespoons balsamic vinegar
- 2 cloves garlic, minced
- salt and pepper to taste

For the herb sauce:

- 1/2 cup fresh parsley, finely chopped
- 1/4 cup fresh basil, finely chopped
- 2 tablespoons olive oil
- juice of 1 lemon
- 1 clove garlic, minced
- salt and pepper to taste

Instructions

1. Preheat your grill or grill pan to medium-high heat.
2. In a small bowl, whisk together olive oil, balsamic vinegar, minced garlic, salt, and pepper. Brush this mixture generously over both sides of the Portobello mushrooms.
3. Place the mushrooms on the grill, gill side down, and cook for about 5-7 minutes on each side, or until they are tender and have grill marks.
4. While the mushrooms are grilling, prepare the herb sauce by combining parsley, basil, olive oil, lemon juice, minced garlic, and a dash of salt and pepper in a bowl. Stir until well mixed.
5. Transfer the cooked mushrooms to a serving platter. Spoon the herb sauce over the mushrooms before serving.
6. Optional tip: For an added flavor boost, let the mushrooms marinate in the olive oil and balsamic mixture for up to an hour before grilling.

Nutritional Information per Serving

- Calories: 180 kcal

- Total Fat: 14 g
- Saturated Fat: 2 g
- Cholesterol: 0 mg
- Sodium: 75 mg (varies based on the use of salt)
- Total Carbohydrates: 10 g
- Dietary Fiber: 2 g
- Sugars: 6 g
- Protein: 4 g

Cauliflower Steaks With Turmeric and Garlic

We're keeping with the steak theme, but we're switching things up a bit by using cauliflower instead of mushrooms. In the previous recipe, we might have had you questioning the concept of the steak already, but this one is just going to blow your mind even further. This dish not only offers you all the health benefits of a DASH-approved dish, but it also showcases how cauliflower can certainly hold its own as the star of a dish. More than anything, this recipe shows that even simple ingredients can transform a meal completely, as long as they're prepared with care and imagination.

Serving Size

- 4

Preparation Time

- 10 minutes

Cooking Time

- 25 minutes

Ingredients

- 2 large heads of cauliflower
- 3 tablespoons olive oil

- 1 teaspoon turmeric
- 2 cloves garlic, minced
- salt and pepper to taste
- fresh parsley or cilantro for garnish

Instructions

1. Preheat the oven to 400 °F (200 °C). Line a baking sheet with parchment paper.
2. Remove the leaves from the cauliflower and cut the heads vertically into thick slices, approximately one-inch thick, to form "steaks." Depending on the size of the cauliflower, you should get about 2 steaks per head.
3. In a small bowl, mix together the olive oil, turmeric, minced garlic, salt, and pepper.
4. Place the cauliflower steaks on the prepared baking sheet. Brush both sides of each steak with the turmeric and garlic oil mixture.
5. Roast in the preheated oven for about 20–25 minutes, or until the cauliflower is tender and the edges are golden and slightly crispy.
6. Serve the cauliflower steaks garnished with fresh parsley or cilantro, if desired.
7. Optional tip: Serve the cauliflower steaks with a side of mixed greens or quinoa for a complete meal.

Nutritional Information per Serving

- Calories: 150 kcal
- Total Fat: 10 g
- Saturated Fat: 1.5 g
- Cholesterol: 0 mg
- Sodium: 30 mg (varies based on the use of salt)
- Total Carbohydrates: 12 g
- Dietary Fiber: 5 g

- Sugars: 5 g
- Protein: 4 g

Zucchini Noodles With Tomato and Basil Sauce

When you first take a bite of this dish, you'll feel as if you're stepping into a garden of flavors. The zucchini noodles might seem like an odd concept at first, but all your hesitations will go away once you actually have that first bite. Of course, you can never go wrong with a classic tomato sauce for a paste, either. Unfortunately, a lot of the ready-made tomato sauces from stores tend to be really high in sodium and preservatives. This recipe will require you to make the sauce from scratch so that you know that you're getting the real thing!

Serving Size

- 4

Preparation Time

- 15 minutes

Cooking Time

- 20 minutes

Ingredients

- 4 large zucchinis
- 1 tablespoon olive oil
- 2 garlic cloves, minced
- 1 small onion, finely chopped
- 2 cups fresh tomatoes, diced (or canned no-salt-added diced tomatoes)
- 1/4 cup fresh basil leaves, chopped
- red pepper flakes to taste

- salt and black pepper to taste
- grated Parmesan cheese (optional)

Instructions

1. Use a spiralizer to turn the zucchinis into noodles. If you don't have a spiralizer, you can use a vegetable peeler to create thin, pasta-like strips.

2. In a large skillet, heat the olive oil over medium heat. Sauté the minced garlic and chopped onion until translucent and fragrant, about 5 minutes.

3. Add the diced tomatoes to the skillet, along with the chopped basil, and a pinch of salt, pepper, and red pepper flakes. Simmer the sauce over medium-low heat for about 10–15 minutes, or until it thickens slightly.

4. While the sauce simmers, place the zucchini noodles in a colander and sprinkle them lightly with salt (if using). Let them sit for about 10 minutes to release excess water, then gently squeeze the noodles to remove moisture.

5. Add the zucchini noodles to the tomato sauce, tossing gently to coat. Cook for an additional 2–3 minutes, or just until the noodles are tender.

6. Serve the zucchini noodles, topped with some grated Parmesan cheese and additional fresh basil.

7. Optional tip: if you prefer a crunchier texture to the zucchini noodles, reduce the cooking time after adding them to the sauce.

Nutritional Information per Serving

- Calories: 120 kcal
- Total Fat: 4 g
- Saturated Fat: 0.5 g
- Cholesterol: 0 mg (without Parmesan cheese)
- Sodium: 25 mg (varies based on the use of salt and cheese)
- Total Carbohydrates: 18 g
- Dietary Fiber: 5 g

- Sugars: 10 g
- Protein: 4 g

Butternut Squash and Black Bean Enchiladas

This next dish certainly has a lot going for it. Nutty. Sweet. Mushy. Grainy. Chewy. Crunchy. There are so many elements to this dish that make it so interesting and fun to eat! More than the fun factor, this dish is also loaded with fiber, vitamins, and minerals that will help make you fitter and stronger. You can prepare these enchiladas ahead of time and refrigerate them until they're ready to bake. This makes them a great option for busy weeknights or meal prep.

Serving Size

- 6

Preparation Time

- 30 minutes

Cooking Time

- 25 minutes

Ingredients

- 1 medium butternut squash, peeled, seeded, and diced into small cubes
- 1 tablespoon olive oil
- 1 can (15 oz) black beans, rinsed and drained
- 1 teaspoon ground cumin
- 1/2 teaspoon chili powder
- 6 whole wheat or corn tortillas
- 2 cups homemade or low-sodium enchilada sauce
- 1 cup shredded low-fat cheese (optional)

- salt and pepper to taste
- fresh cilantro for garnish
- Greek yogurt or sour cream for serving (optional)

Instructions

1. Preheat your oven to 375 °F (190 °C). Toss the diced butternut squash with olive oil, salt, and pepper on a baking sheet. Roast for about 20 minutes, or until tender and lightly caramelized.

2. In a large bowl, combine the roasted butternut squash, black beans, cumin, and chili powder, mixing well to combine.

3. Spread a thin layer of enchilada sauce on the bottom of a baking dish.

4. Warm the tortillas according to the package instructions to make them more pliable. Divide the squash and bean mixture evenly among the tortillas, rolling them up and placing them seam-side down in the baking dish.

5. Pour the remaining enchilada sauce over the rolled tortillas, covering them thoroughly. Sprinkle with shredded cheese.

6. Bake in the preheated oven for about 25 minutes, or until the enchiladas are heated through and the cheese is melted and bubbly.

7. Garnish with fresh cilantro and serve with a dollop of Greek yogurt or sour cream on the side.

Nutritional Information per Serving

- Calories: 350 kcal
- Total Fat: 9 g
- Saturated Fat: 2 g
- Cholesterol: 10 mg (with low-fat cheese)
- Sodium: 300 mg (varies with enchilada sauce and cheese)
- Total Carbohydrates: 55 g
- Dietary Fiber: 10 g

- Sugars: 5 g
- Protein: 15 g

Spicy Stir-Fried Tofu With Vegetables

Asia is home to some of the best cooking techniques and culinary philosophies in the world, and this dish is a perfect example of Asian culinary genius. This spicy stir-fried tofu packs just enough punch to invigorate your tastebuds with a variety of textures that keep the entire meal interesting. With this dish, you'll receive a rainbow of vegetables that offer a lot of bang for the buck when it comes to your daily dose of vitamins and minerals.

Serving Size

- 4

Preparation Time

- 15 minutes

Cooking Time

- 10 minutes

Ingredients

- 1 block (14 oz) firm tofu, pressed and cut into cubes
- 2 tablespoons low-sodium soy sauce
- 1 tablespoon sesame oil
- 1 tablespoon chili paste (adjust to taste)
- 2 garlic cloves, minced
- 1 inch ginger, minced
- 2 cups broccoli florets
- 1 red bell pepper, sliced

- 1 yellow bell pepper, sliced
- 1 cup snap peas
- 1 carrot, julienned
- 2 green onions, sliced for garnish
- sesame seeds for garnish

Instructions

1. In a large bowl, toss the tofu cubes with 1 tablespoon of low-sodium soy sauce. Set aside to marinate for at least 10 minutes.

2. Heat the sesame oil in a large skillet or wok over medium-high heat. Add the marinated tofu and stir-fry until golden brown on all sides, about 5–7 minutes. Remove the tofu from the skillet and set aside.

3. In the same skillet, add the chili paste, minced garlic, and ginger. Stir-fry for about 30 seconds until fragrant.

4. Add the broccoli, bell peppers, snap peas, and carrot to the skillet. Stir-fry for about 3–4 minutes, or until the vegetables are tender-crisp.

5. Return the tofu to the skillet. Add the remaining tablespoon of low-sodium soy sauce and toss everything together until the sauce coats the tofu and vegetables well and heats through.

6. Serve the stir-fried tofu and vegetables, garnished with sliced green onions and sesame seeds.

Nutritional Information per Serving

- Calories: 200 kcal
- Total Fat: 9 g
- Saturated Fat: 1 g
- Cholesterol: 0 mg
- Sodium: 300 mg
- Total Carbohydrates: 18 g

- Dietary Fiber: 4 g
- Sugars: 6 g
- Protein: 12 g

Balsamic Glazed Beetroot and Goat Cheese Salad

Introduce a burst of flavor and color to your meal with this innovative take on a beetroot and goat cheese salad. It's a vibrant dish that boldly combines the earthy notes of roasted beetroots with the rich and creamy tang of goat cheese. A sweet balsamic reduction then perfectly tops off all of this.

Serving Size

- 4

Preparation Time

- 15 minutes

Cooking Time

- 30 minutes

Ingredients

- 4 medium beetroots, peeled and diced
- 1 tablespoon olive oil
- salt and pepper to taste
- 4 tablespoons balsamic vinegar
- 1 teaspoon honey
- 1/2 cup walnuts, toasted and chopped
- 1/2 cup crumbled goat cheese
- Mixed salad greens (such as arugula and spinach)

- Fresh mint leaves, for garnish

Instructions

1. Preheat your oven to 375 °F (190 °C). Mix the diced beetroots with olive oil, and season lightly with salt and black pepper. Arrange them on a baking sheet and roast for about 30 minutes, or until they are tender and slightly caramelized.

2. While the beetroots are in the oven, start making the balsamic glaze. In a small saucepan, mix balsamic vinegar with honey. Let it simmer on low heat until it thickens and reduces to roughly half of the initial volume, achieving a syrupy consistency.

3. In a large salad bowl, lay out the mixed greens. Add the roasted beetroots, toasted walnuts, and crumbled goat cheese on top.

4. Pour the balsamic reduction over the salad just before you're ready to serve.

5. For a refreshing finish, garnish with fresh mint leaves.

Nutritional Information per Serving

- Calories: 250 kcal

- Total Fat: 15 g

- Saturated Fat: 4 g

- Cholesterol: 13 mg

- Sodium: 180 mg

- Total Carbohydrates: 20 g

- Dietary Fiber: 3 g

- Sugars: 16 g

- Protein: 8 g

Grilled Portobello Mushroom Burgers

Grilled Portobello Mushroom Burgers offer a tasty, heart-healthy choice that fits perfectly with DASH and vegetarian principles, making them a great alternative to traditional beef burgers. These burgers feature large portobello mushrooms known for their satisfying texture and rich taste, are expertly grilled, and are served with various fresh toppings on a whole-grain bun. It's a dish that satisfies anyone's craving for a burger while providing essential nutrients and avoiding the saturated fats commonly found in red meat.

Serving Size

- 4

Preparation Time

- 10 minutes

Cooking Time

- 10 minutes

Ingredients

- 4 large portobello mushroom caps, stems, and gills removed
- 2 tablespoons balsamic vinegar
- 2 tablespoons olive oil
- 1 garlic clove, minced
- salt and pepper to taste
- 4 whole-grain burger buns
- 1 ripe avocado, sliced
- 1 tomato, sliced
- 1 small red onion, thinly sliced
- 1 cup fresh spinach leaves
- Optional: mustard or low-sodium ketchup

Instructions

1. In a small bowl, combine balsamic vinegar, olive oil, and minced garlic. Season lightly with salt and black pepper.

2. Coat each mushroom cap with the mixture, ensuring coverage on both sides. Preheat the grill to medium-high. Grill the mushrooms for about 5 minutes per side, until tender with grill marks.

3. Optionally, toast the whole-grain buns on the grill.

4. To build the burgers, place a grilled mushroom on the bottom half of each bun. Add avocado, tomato, red onion, and spinach.

5. To taste, add mustard or low-sodium ketchup.

6. Top with the other half of the bun and serve immediately.

Nutritional Information per Serving

- Calories: 200 kcal

- Total Fat: 7 g

- Saturated Fat: 1 g

- Cholesterol: 60 mg

- Sodium: 250 mg (varies based on the use of salt and capers)

- Total Carbohydrates: 2 g

- Dietary Fiber: 0 g

- Sugars: 0 g

- Protein: 30 g

Measurement Charts

Dry Measurements

Cups	Tablespoons	Ounces	Milliliters
1 cup	16 Tbsp.	8 oz.	237 ml
¾ cup	12 Tbsp.	6 oz.	177 ml
2/3 cup	11 Tbsp.	5 oz.	158 ml
½ cup	8 Tbsp.	4 oz.	118 ml
1/3 cup	5.5 Tbsp.	3 oz.	79 ml
¼ cup	4 Tbsp.	2 oz.	59 ml
1/8 cup	2 Tbsp.	1 oz.	30 ml
1/16 cup	1 Tbsp.	½ oz.	15 ml

Liquid Measurements

Cups	Ounces	Liters
8 cups or 4 pints	64 oz.	1.9 liters
4 cups or 2 pints	32 oz.	0.95 liters
2 cups or 1 pint	16 oz.	480 ml
1 cup	8 oz.	240 ml
½ cup	4 oz.	120 ml
¼ cup	2 oz.	60 ml

Temperatures

Fahrenheit (F)	Celsius (C)
500°F	260°C
450°F	230°C
425°F	220°C
400°F	200°C
375°F	190°C
350°F	180°C
325°F	160°C
300°F	150°C
250°F	121°C
200°F	93°C
150°F	65°C
100°F	37°C

Weight Measurements

Imperial	Metric
½ oz.	15 g
1 oz.	29 g
2 oz.	57 g
3 oz.	85 g

4 oz.	113 g
5 oz.	141 g
6 oz.	170 g
8 oz.	227 g
10 oz.	283 g
12 oz.	340 g
13 oz.	369 g
14 oz.	397 g
15 oz.	425 g
16 oz. or 1lb	453 g

Conclusion

You've reached the end of the cookbook, but it's just the start of your journey into the world of DASH dieting! Despite the original development of the diet to target high blood pressure, it ultimately serves as an inclusive, flexible, and non-restrictive diet program that many people can benefit from. We made this cookbook with the belief that achieving a healthier lifestyle doesn't require boring and bland meals. You don't have to sacrifice the joy of eating in order to achieve your wellness goals. Hopefully, the dishes in this cookbook will inspire you to seek creative ways to satisfy your gastronomic cravings without having to compromise your health and wellness.

Keep in mind that the ingredients and instructions listed in these recipes are merely suggestions. You're free to get as creative as you want with your dishes. Experiment with different combinations of spices, vegetables, proteins, and cooking techniques. Use these recipes as inspiration to create dishes that not only nourish your body but also bring vibrance and color to your life.

References

15-Minute spicy shrimp and quinoa. (2021, February 22). Her Highness, Hungry Me. https://hh-hm.com/spicy-shrimp-and-quinoa/

Bryan, L. (2020, August 24). *Mediterranean chickpea salad.* Downshiftology. https://downshiftology.com/recipes/mediterranean-chickpea-salad/

Bull, N. (2016, October 14). *Creamy dijon rosemary chicken.* Salt & Lavender. https://www.saltandlavender.com/creamy-dijon-rosemary-chicken/

Butternut squash black bean enchiladas. (2015, December). Minimalist Baker. https://minimalistbaker.com/butternut-squash-black-bean-enchiladas/

Carrie. (2022, August 1). *Baked apple chips.* Carrie's Experimental Kitchen. https://www.carriesexperimentalkitchen.com/cinnamon-apple-chips/

Cary, C. (2020, March 27). *Sheet pan maple soy glazed salmon.* Eat with Clarity. https://eatwithclarity.com/maple-glazed-salmon/

Cauliflower steak with turmeric and garlic recipe. (n.d.). Food. Retrieved April 4, 2024, from https://www.food.com/recipe/cauliflower-steak-with-turmeric-and-garlic-527703

Challa, H. J., & Uppaluri, K. R. (2023, January 23). *DASH diet (dietary approaches to stop hypertension).* Nih.gov; StatPearls Publishing. https://www.ncbi.nlm.nih.gov/books/NBK482514/

DASH diet: Healthy eating to lower your blood pressure. (2021, June 25). Mayo Clinic. https://www.mayoclinic.org/healthy-lifestyle/nutrition-and-healthy-eating/in-depth/dash-diet/art-20048456

Gaewski, R. (2023, May 3). *Sweet potato and black bean burritos recipe by tasty.* Tasty.co. https://tasty.co/recipe/sweet-potato-and-black-bean-burritos

Gavin, J. (2021). *Spicy tofu stir-fry.* Simply Recipes. https://www.simplyrecipes.com/spicy-tofu-stir-fry-recipe-5115374

Grater, L. (2014, July 10). *Simple poached egg and avocado toast.* Pinchofyum.com. https://pinchofyum.com/simple-poached-egg-avocado-toast

Grater, L. (2016, July 19). *Berry chia overnight oats.* Pinch of Yum. https://pinchofyum.com/chia-overnight-oats

Grater, L. (2020, June 15). *Nourishing quinoa breakfast bowl*. Green Healthy Cooking. https://greenhealthycooking.com/quinoa-breakfast-bowl/

Grilled lamb chops with yogurt mint sauce recipe. (n.d.). Meatwave.com. Retrieved April 4, 2024, from https://meatwave.com/recipes/grilled-lamb-chops-with-yogurt-mint-sauce-recipe

Homolka, G. (2022, January 8). *Mushroom-Spinach scrambled eggs*. Skinnytaste. https://www.skinnytaste.com/mushroom-spinach-scrambled-eggs/

House, G. (2021, January 14). *Savory roasted chickpeas*. World of Vegan. https://www.worldofvegan.com/roasted-chickpeas/

Jennings, K.-A. (2017, May 9). *Best foods for A healthy brain and improved memory*. Healthline; Healthline Media. https://www.healthline.com/nutrition/11-brain-foods#faq

Karadsheh, S. (2022, January 16). *Mediterranean spicy lentil soup*. The Mediterranean Dish. https://www.themediterraneandish.com/mediterranean-spicy-spinach-lentil-soup/

Lemon and herb baked salmon. (2022, June 24). Little Health Bunny. https://www.littlehealthbunny.com/blog/2022/6/24/lemon-and-herb-baked-salmon

Lichty, M. (2013, September 13). *Roasted vegetable pita sandwich recipe*. Two Peas & Their Pod. https://www.twopeasandtheirpod.com/roasted-vegetable-pita-sandwich/

Lynn, T. (2008, January 15). *Curried chicken lettuce wraps*. Allrecipes. https://www.allrecipes.com/recipe/283430/curried-chicken-lettuce-wraps/

Mandal, A. (2010, May 19). *The DASH-Sodium study*. News-Medical. https://www.news-medical.net/health/The-DASH-Sodium-study.aspx

Mansaray, Z. (2014, July 2). *Grilled vegetable quinoa salad*. A Classic Twist. https://aclassictwist.com/grilled-vegetable-quinoa-salad/

Marie. (2016, December 21). *Quinoa and black bean stuffed bell peppers*. Yay! For Food. https://www.yayforfood.com/recipes/quinoa-and-black-bean-stuffed-bell-peppers/

McKenney, S. (2024, January 4). *Thick & hearty minestrone soup*. Sally's Baking Addiction. https://sallysbakingaddiction.com/minestrone-soup/

Melanie. (2020, November 18). *Roasted brussels sprouts with balsamic glaze*. Garnish & Glaze. https://www.garnishandglaze.com/roasted-brussels-sprouts-with-balsamic-glaze/

Miller, S. (2024, January 26). *Quinoa salad*. The Mediterranean Dish. https://www.themediterraneandish.com/quinoa-salad/

Moore, M. (2016, July 7). *Zucchini noodles with tomato, basil and parmesan*. Marisa Moore Nutrition. https://marisamoore.com/zucchini-noodles-tomato-basil-parmesan/

Mullins, B. (2020, August 30). *No bake energy balls*. Eating Bird Food. https://www.eatingbirdfood.com/no-bake-energy-balls/

Mullins, B. (2023, June 2). *Banana almond butter smoothie*. Eating Bird Food. https://www.eatingbirdfood.com/almond-butter-smoothie/

Nora. (2023, August 31). *Eggplant curry*. Nora Cooks. https://www.noracooks.com/chickpea-and-eggplant-curry/

Peaches & cottage cheese parfait recipe. (2016, October 5). Recipes. https://www.postconsumerbrands.com/recipes/grab-go-cottage-crunch/

Portobello "steaks" topped with spinach and herbs. (2012, March 12). Out of the Ordinary. https://outoftheordinaryfood.com/2012/03/12/portobello-steaks-topped-with-spinach-and-herbs/

Rene. (2022, August 19). *Mediterranean quinoa wraps*. This Savory Vegan. https://www.thissavoryvegan.com/mediterranean-quinoa-wraps/

Sanford, A. (2022, July 5). *Greek yogurt parfait (make ahead recipe)*. Foolproof Living. https://foolproofliving.com/layered-yogurt-parfait/

Sharma, N. (2022, October 9). *Spiced roasted pumpkin seeds*. Nik Sharma Cooks. https://niksharmacooks.com/spiced-roasted-pumpkin-seeds/

Sheet-Pan honey-balsamic pork chop dinner. (2018, January 9). BettyCrocker.com. https://www.bettycrocker.com/recipes/sheet-pan-honey-balsamic-pork-chop-dinner/a2eb0eb5-a5dc-41ba-8173-d5b0db56a5cf

Smith, J. (2019, January 29). *Dark chocolate almond energy bites*. Inquiring Chef. https://inquiringchef.com/dark-chocolate-almond-energy-bites/

Taylor, K. (2018, November 29). *Whole wheat banana pancakes*. Cookie and Kate. https://cookieandkate.com/whole-wheat-banana-pancakes-recipe/

Tuna-and-White-Bean salad recipe. (2017, May 31). Food & Wine. https://www.foodandwine.com/recipes/tuna-and-white-bean-salad

Turkey and avocado club salad. (2021, May 12). The Salad Whisperer. https://thesaladwhisperer.com/turkey-and-avocado-club-salad/

Understanding the DASH diet. (n.d.). Medlineplus.gov. https://medlineplus.gov/ency/patientinstructions/000784.htm

Voicu, M. (2020, November 2). *Herb roasted chicken & veggies (paleo, keto & whole30).* Healyeatsreal.com. https://healyeatsreal.com/roasted-chicken-veggies/

Welch, S. (2020, February 25). *Beef and broccoli stir fry.* Dinner at the Zoo. https://www.dinneratthezoo.com/beef-and-broccoli-stir-fry/

Workman, K. (2022, June 19). *Spinach feta omelet.* The Mom 100. https://themom100.com/recipe/spinach-feta-omelet/

World Health Organization. (2024, March 1). *Obesity and overweight.* World Health Organization; World Health Organization. https://www.who.int/news-room/fact-sheets/detail/obesity-and-overweight

Printed in Great Britain
by Amazon